BASIC SAILING

With 214 illustrations

The American National Red Cross

Washington, D.C.

Library of Congress Catalog Card No. 66-4077

Basic Sailing has been developed as a text for the American Red Cross sailing course by Charles W. Russell, director of Safety Programs.

The American Red Cross acknowledges with appreciation the permission granted by Doubleday & Co., Inc., to reproduce the class insignia contained in *The Sailboat Classes of North America*, by Fessenden Blanchard, and the information provided by the Plymouth Cordage Company concerning the tensile strength of the different types and sizes of rope. Special acknowledgment is extended to the United States Coast Guard for the information provided on Rules of the Road and lighting and equipment regulations. The glossary was selected from "Naval Terms and Definitions," Knight's *Modern Seamanship*, 11th edition. Copyright 1945, D. Van Nostrand Company, Inc., Princeton, N.J.

The Small Craft Safety program of the American National Red Cross, for which this book is a teaching text, stems from the Congressional charter provision that the organization shall devise and carry on measures for relieving and preventing accidents and suffering. Through this program the Red Cross helps to prevent injury or the loss of life by teaching people the skills necessary for their greater enjoyment of water activities.

CONTENTS

BASIC SAILING

The history of exploration, conquest, trade, and culture is also the story of man's fascination with the wind and the sea and his often heroic attempts to harness and tame these powerful forces of nature for his own purposes. The first prehistoric "sailor" probably ventured afloat on a log or a raft. Later man developed the dugout canoe. He soon found that it was easier to pole or paddle with the wind, and it is almost certain, long before the dawn of history, that he made "sails" of tree branches, skins, or woven reeds to propel his craft before a favorable breeze.

PHOENICIAN TRADER

The earliest records of sail craft are found in the carvings that decorate some of the 5,000-year-old tombs of the Pharaohs. A single squaresail and oars were used for propulsion. The Phoenicians, who colonized the Western Mediterranean, built their seagoing galleys based on the Egyptian pattern and also developed the art of navigation. Later, the Assyrians and then the Greeks and Romans enlarged and improved the design of the galley. This craft often exceeded 125 feet in length and usually had, in addition to a large squaresail, two or three banks of oars pulled by galley slaves. Formidable torpedo-like weapons were made of these naval vessels by the addition of an underwater prow for ramming enemy ships. The Vikings, during their piratical raids in Western Europe and the Mediterranean, saw and adopted the Roman squaresail and made legendary voyages to North America in their "long ships" 500 years before Columbus reached the West Indies in the *Santa Maria*.

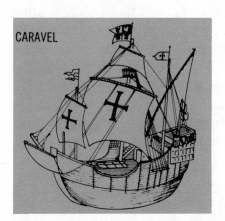

CARAVEL

The caravels of Columbus' day had three or four masts. Squaresails, which have never been equalled for downwind sailing, were carried on the foremast and lateen sails on the other masts. The lateen, probably of Moorish origin, enabled the boats to work to windward and made possible the designing of larger and more maneuverable vessels that relied on wind power alone for propulsion.

The lateens were the forerunner of the more efficient "fore and aft" sails, but the squarerigger dominated the golden age of sail during the clipper ship era. The devel-

CLIPPER

opment of the clippers was favored by competition for world markets and the discovery and charting of sea lanes where the predictable "trade winds" blew for most of the year. The clippers were designed for speed and built primarily for the lucrative China tea trade, but after gold was discovered in California, many American clippers carried men and supplies around the Horn to San Francisco before heading across the Pacific. They were driven hard by able and sometimes ruthless skippers and made impressive records even by today's standards. The *Flying Cloud*, for example, in 1851 sailed the 17,600 miles between New York and San Francisco at an average speed of over 10 miles per hour and logged over 420 miles in one 24-hour period.

The commercial sailing vessels have disappeared except in some spots of the world where competition and speed are of little consequence. The oyster-dredging skipjacks of Chesapeake Bay are the last of the working sail craft in the United States, only because of a state law prohibiting the use of powerboats for dredging. But, paradoxically, more people are sailing today than ever before. Young and old, they sail for recreation, relaxation, and adventure. They sail in crafts ranging from prams or dinghies costing a few dollars to "cup" defenders and challengers in which many millions have been invested. The urge to sail and the lure of the sea have not been dimmed by technical achievements and journeys into space.

SAILBOAT TYPES

Recreational sailing falls into three main classifications: racing, cruising, and day sailing. A great variety of boat hulls has been developed to meet the specific requirements of each category. The types can be broadly classified, with some overlap, as (1) sailing prams and dinghies, (2) day sailers, (3) racing classes, (4) cruising classes, and (5) a special group consisting of board boats, canoes, and the multihulled catamarans and trimarans.

Although day sailers and cruising craft are often raced in competition with other boats of the same type, or under a time handicap arrangement, the day sailer is essentially a family boat designed for a safe, comfortable day afloat, whereas a cruising boat is built for sailing in comfort and safety for extended periods of time. The racing craft, on the other hand, is a highly efficient machine that is rigged, tuned, and sailed to cover distance in the shortest possible time. Obviously, no single hull design is best for all purposes and conditions. The designer must sacrifice comfort to gain speed or perhaps compromise on speed to increase stability. He may alter sail plans to compensate for regional wind conditions or he may have to substitute materials and economize on labor to lower production costs. In short, boat designs are a combination of compromises arrived at by the naval architect after a thorough study of intended use balanced by all the variables involved, including cost and upkeep. Within this framework the designer works to produce a hull shape and sail plan that are more efficient than those of existing comparable models and yet retain an appearance that is pleasing to the eye and acceptable to prospective purchasers.

SAILBOAT CLASSES

One-Design Boats

Two or more craft built to the same design and specifications are known as *one-design* boats. Individual owners of one-design sailboats often form an association and race as a one-design class. Theoretically, all the craft in a one-

SNIPE CLASS

design class are identical, and racing results are decided on skill alone. The strict control that each association exercises over hull, sail, and gear specifications tends to stabilize the purchase price and the operating cost and provides a reasonable assurance, among the more popular classes, of a higher resale value if the boat has a good racing record. One-design associations have multiplied rapidly since World War II, and their promotion of sailing activities at local, national, and international levels has greatly stimulated interest and participation in all classifications of sailing. Such sailboats as Penguins, Snipes, and Stars are popular one-design classes.

DECKED
SAILING CANOE

Development Classes

There are several sailboat associations in which designers

or owners are allowed to make changes or modifications within specified limits of length, beam, weight, sail area, etc. The plan provides an opportunity to test ideas and gear under racing conditions in competition with other craft of the same basic design. These "development classes," as they are known, appeal particularly to those who are interested in research and experimentation. Moths, decked sailing canoes, Suicides, and International 14s are examples of development classes.

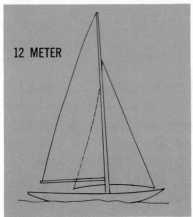

12 METER

Rating Classes

Racing sailboats such as the 12 Meters used in the America's Cup competition race without time handicaps, although they may not be exactly alike in shape. In the rating classes individual designs are based on a complex but flexible mathematical formula that is applied to weight, girth, length, sail area, and other measurements that determine speed potential. The designer essentially starts with the *answer* to an equation, be it 6, 8, 10, or 12 meters, and juggles the components around that, in his estimation, will make for a faster boat. With the exception of the Cup defenders, the one-designs have largely replaced the rating classes in sailing competition. In addition to the meter boats, the "letter" classes of J, M, R, etc., are examples of the rating classes.

Measurement Rule

Various measurement rules have been developed for rating sailboats of different design so that they may race together on a handicapped basis or on equal terms. The best known rule is that of the Cruising Club of America, a rule that is used in most long distance races in North America. The boats racing under CCA rules must be measured and rated by a person accredited by the Club.

SAILBOAT HULLS AND THEIR CHARACTERISTICS

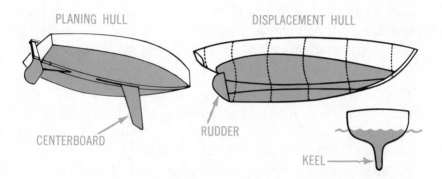

PLANING HULL   DISPLACEMENT HULL

CENTERBOARD

RUDDER

KEEL

A few racing sailboat hulls, under optimum conditions, are designed to plane on the surface of the water in the manner of most outboard motorboats, but the vast majority are displacement hulls, which displace a volume of water equal to their total weight as they float or move through the water. Unlike a powerboat, however, a sailing hull must perform efficiently under the variables of wind force, wind direction or heading, and wave action and at the same time resist the tendency to capsize as a result of wind pressure on the sails when on certain headings.

The resistance of the hull to capsizing or heeling over is known as *transverse stability* and it is a key element in the design of a sailboat. A boat is said to be "stiff" or "tender" on the basis of its resistance to heeling.

Stability is determined by hull form and weight distribution or location of the craft's center of gravity. A beamy hull or a heavy keel or a combination of both will increase stability but will tend to decrease performance in light airs and while running downwind. Only with experience

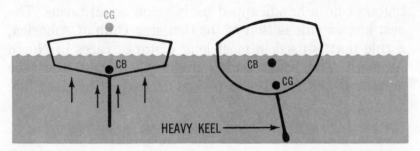

CG

CB

CB

CG

HEAVY KEEL ⟶

and a knowledge of the environmental conditions where the boat will be generally sailed can a designer develop a hull form and sail plan for specific purposes and conditions.

The location of a sailboat's center of gravity (CG) will vary with the weight and disposition of ballast, if any, as well as the weight and distribution of the crew and all gear that may be aboard. Theoretically, the center of gravity is a point where the total weight of the boat and everything aboard could be centered and have the same effect on the hull in its relation to the water. Since stability is directly related to the location of the center of gravity, as well as to hull form, it is imperative that the CG be as low as possible to avoid excessive heeling or capsizing.

The supporting pressure on the hull that resists and equalizes downward weight (displacement) can also be replaced, theoretically, by a single point that is called the center of buoyancy (CB).

When the boat rests in any position of athwartship trim caused by shifting the weight aboard, the CG and the CB lie in the same vertical plane. A change in trim or heeling caused by wind pressure on the sails, however, will be resisted by the upward pressure of the center of buoyancy as it shifts with the change in shape of the underwater hull form.

The resisting force is called the *righting moment* and it expresses the contribution made by the hull form to the stability of the craft. Note that the underwater shape of

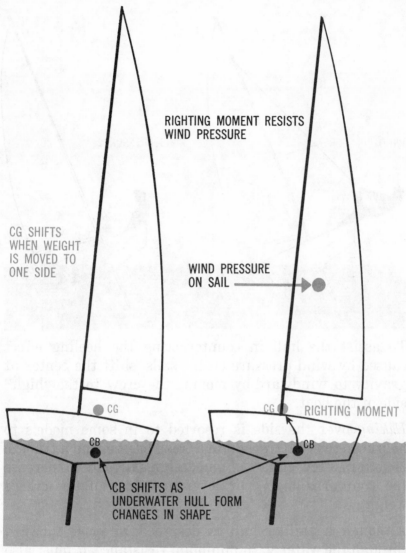

RIGHTING MOMENT RESISTS
WIND PRESSURE

CG SHIFTS
WHEN WEIGHT
IS MOVED TO
ONE SIDE

WIND PRESSURE
ON SAIL

CG

CG   RIGHTING MOMENT

CB

CB

CB SHIFTS AS
UNDERWATER HULL FORM
CHANGES IN SHAPE

a round bottom hull has little or no change when heeled and consequently little or no initial stability unless a heavy keel is added.

Boat hulls move through the water with less resistance when they remain upright or nearly so. The wetted surface, which produces drag, on some models can be reduced, however, by heeling the boats to leeward; but, when the angle of heel is excessive, the underwater hull shape is generally unfavorably altered. Also, the effective sail area is smaller and speed is reduced.

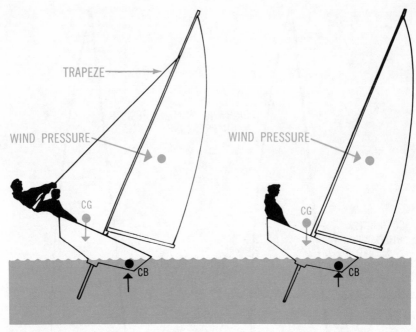

To assist the hull in counteracting the heeling effect caused by wind pressure on the sails, shift the center of gravity to windward by moving the crew to the "high" side of the boat.

Hiking over the side is resorted to in some models to help keep the boat upright in a fresh breeze, and a trapeze is used in a few classes of one-design sailboats to increase the counterbalancing or leverage effect of the crew's weight.

Although a sailing hull is designed to move forward through the water with minimum resistance, it must also offer the greatest possible resistance to sideways movement. Resistance to moving broadside or making leeway through the water is known as *lateral resistance*. Unless such resistance is provided for, sailing across, or at an angle into, the wind would be impossible.

A sailboat hull generally depends upon underwater vertical plane surfaces that are attached to, or are a part of, the hull to provide sufficient lateral resistance. The keel

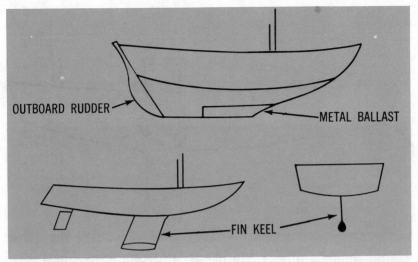

OUTBOARD RUDDER

METAL BALLAST

FIN KEEL

is the "backbone" of a boat's hull, and in sailing hulls it is usually extended downward to increase lateral resistance. Ballast in the form of lead or other metal is often added to the lower edge of the keel to increase transverse stability. Some racing models have a metal fin attached

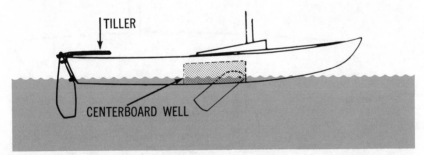

TILLER

CENTERBOARD WELL

to the keel, which, in turn, is ballasted with metal in the shape of a torpedo or a bulb.

Having a hinged centerboard is the most common method of providing lateral resistance. The board can be adjusted to give the amount of resistance needed for any heading, or it can be raised completely when sailing before the wind, when making leeway is no problem. Besides decreasing drag by reducing the wetted (underwater) surface area, the raised board also permits the boat to be maneuvered in waters too shallow for fixed-keel boats of comparable size.

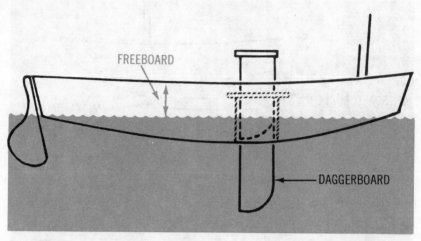

Daggerboards offer a simple arrangement for small sailboats. They require less space than a centerboard but are more awkward to adjust and handle in light airs and shallow water.

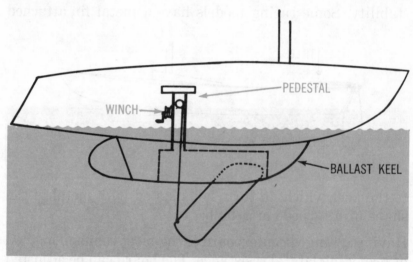

A keel-centerboard combination is used in many popular ocean racing-cruising sailboats. The board is housed in the shallow ballast-keel and can be lowered as needed when sailing to windward.

A canoe rigged for sailing and some prams, as, for example, sabots, use leeboards to prevent making leeway. Today, prototypes of old Dutch sailing vessels also em-

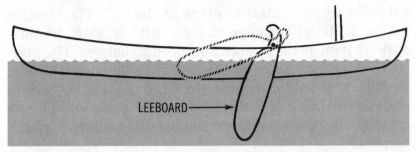

LEEBOARD——→

ploy large leeboards; in most instances only the board on the lee side is lowered when sailing on the wind.

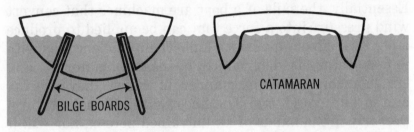

BILGE BOARDS

CATAMARAN

The fast sailing scows are fitted with bilge boards, one on each side of the keel. The boards are fashioned like a centerboard, but the arrangement provides for good lateral resistance when the boats are heeled well over on their sides.

Some sailing craft, such as catamarans, depend on the flat side surface on the hull form to prevent making leeway.

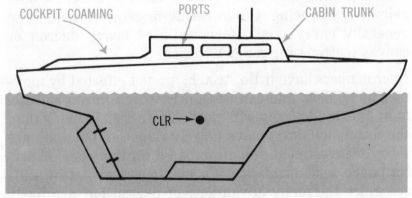

COCKPIT COAMING   PORTS   CABIN TRUNK

CLR——→●

As in the case of the boat's gravity and buoyancy, lateral resistance can also be centered at a specific point. The point, referred to as the center of lateral resistance

(CLR), lies in or near the geometrical center of the vertical underwater centerline plane of the hull. The location of the CLR will change slightly with a shift in fore-and-aft trim as the underwater profile changes. The pressure of the bow wave on the leeward side when the boat is underway will also cause the CLR to shift. As will be seen later, the CLR is directly related to the sail plan in establishing the balance or the handling characteristics of a craft.

SAILS

Essentially, the sails of a boat are machines that convert wind pressure into a force that can be applied to produce a physical effect on a boat's hull. Their efficiency, as with any machine, is determined by design, material, and craftmanship, plus the manner in which they are operated and cared for. The finest sail will not perform properly in the hands of an untrained person, nor will it withstand abuse and neglect. On the other hand, if it is expertly handled and maintained it will operate at peak efficiency for many years.

Sail-Making Material

Most sails used in recreational and competitive sailing are made of synthetic material: dacron for regular, or *working*, sails and nylon for the large *light* sails used primarily in racing. Ocean racing or cruising boats also generally carry small *storm* sails of heavy dacron or canvas (cotton) for rough weather.

Dacron fibers have little stretch, are not effected by moisture or mildew, and can be tightly woven into a smooth, light fabric ideal for sail cloth. Their cost is more than the cotton sails they have largely replaced, but they are a better investment when compared on the basis of performance and durability. Former users of cotton sails recognize the many advantages of dacron but are likely to object to the glossy sheen of the fabric and its slick, slippery qualities that make it rather difficult to furl or to bag.

14

Nylon fabric is used almost exclusively for making the light sails of racing craft that are used in addition to the working sails.

Care of Sails

Synthetic sails are affected by long exposure to sunlight and should be removed from the spars when the boat is not in use, or protected with sail covers. Fold small sails

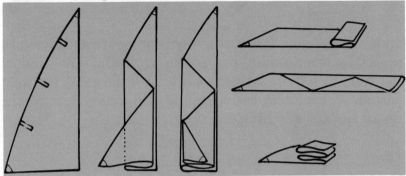

smoothly to avoid wrinkling the surface of the material, for an uneven surface in light air will cause turbulence in the air flow across the sail. The slides should remain outside of the fold so that possible chafing of the material can be avoided. Remove the *battens* and thoroughly dry the sails before folding and bagging. Battens are usually made of thin slats of white ash, although plastic is becoming popular. They should be an inch or so shorter than the pocket and tapered wafer thin at the forward end so that they will blend into the slight curve of the sail. If they are too long or stiff, a break in the curvature of the sail will be noted in a line along the forward edge of the pockets. Sand the battens, especially the edges and corners, to prevent chafe, and waterproof them with several coats of varnish.

The sail bag should be hung in a cool, dry room or locker where air circulation is good. Keep the sails clean and occasionally flush the salt from those used around salt-water areas. Particles of salt in the material will absorb moisture from the atmosphere and add weight to the sail.

Chafing is the main hazard for sails when the boat is

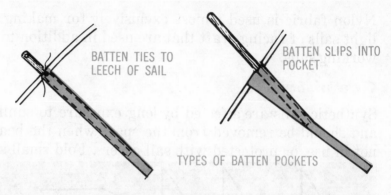

BATTEN TIES TO LEECH OF SAIL

BATTEN SLIPS INTO POCKET

TYPES OF BATTEN POCKETS

under way. Avoid friction against spreaders and shrouds, especially when sailing before the wind, and do not allow the sails to luff in a breeze while at a mooring for long periods of time. Excessive luffing will cause wear of the fibers and the stitching.

Types of Sails

Only a few sail types and methods for rigging them that were developed in the long history of sailing have survived the advent of the air age and the relatively new science of aerodynamics.

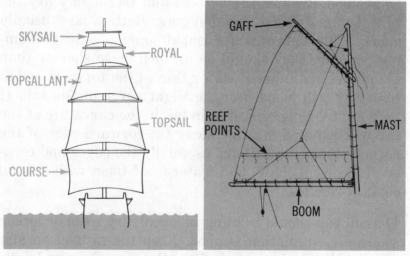

SKYSAIL

ROYAL

TOPGALLANT

TOPSAIL

COURSE

GAFF

REEF POINTS

MAST

BOOM

The squaresail, which powered the famous clippers and Australian grainships, is now found only on a few naval training vessels, and the once common gaff-headed sail is rarely seen on a modern craft.

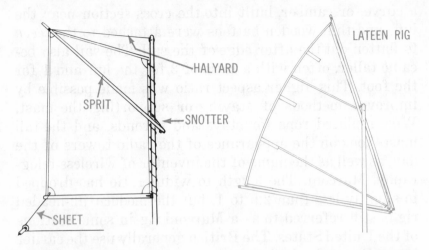

LATEEN RIG

HALYARD

SPRIT

SNOTTER

SHEET

Modern versions of the ancient lateen rigs of the Mediterranean Sea and the Indian Ocean and also the sliding gunter and spritsail rigs are still in use on a variety of small craft, chiefly because of the simplicity of the rigs; but of the older basic types, only the "fore and aft" rigged triangular sails have withstood the tests of time and science.

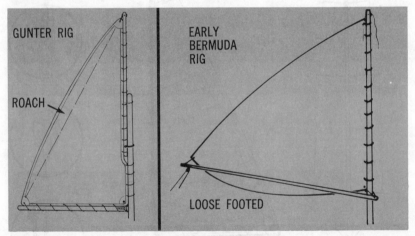

GUNTER RIG

ROACH

EARLY
BERMUDA
RIG

LOOSE FOOTED

The foot and the luff, or hoist, of the earlier triangular Bermuda rig, from which the modern "jib-headed" sail has evolved, were nearly the same length; but early in the twentieth century it was found that the efficiency of the sail could be improved by applying in its design the recently discovered aerodynamic principles of bird and plane flight. The sail became more wing-like in form, with a curve, or camber, built into the cross section near the luff, and thin wooden battens were attached to the *leech* to flatten out the after edge of the sail. The sail also became taller, often with a ratio of 3 for the luff and 1 for the foot. This higher aspect ratio was made possible by improved methods of staying or supporting the mast. Wire replaced rope for stays and shrouds, and the tall masts took on the appearance of the radio towers of the day, as well as the name of the inventor of wireless telegraphy, Marconi. The length to width ratio has dropped to slightly less than 2.5 to 1, but the modern jib-headed rig is still referred to as a Marconi rig in some sections of the United States. The British generally use the earlier term "Bermuda rig."

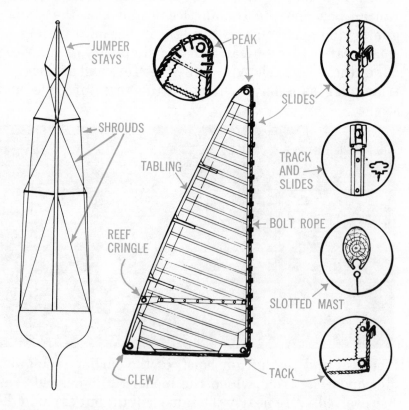

A sailboat is literally pushed along by the pressure on its sail when running before the wind, but other forces come into play on the sails and hull when the heading is changed to sail across or into the wind.

A well-designed boat, properly handled, can sail into the wind at an angle of about 45 degrees. Some of the finely tuned racing craft can "point" a little higher, but the average sailboat will begin to stall if "pinched" closer than 45 degrees.

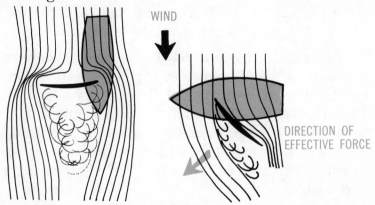

The positive pressure of the wind against the face of the sail decreases as the angle of the sail to the wind decreases. The diminishing force, however, continues to exert pressure at right angles to the sail's surface.

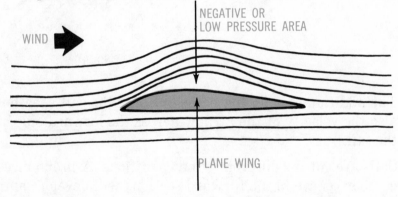

The tendency for the boat to move sideways with the wind is resisted by water pressure on the hull and other vertical underwater plane surfaces such as the keel or the centerboard. The "squeeze" that is exerted on the hull by two forces—one pushing and the other resisting—is often compared to pinching a melon seed between the thumb and the index finger. The seed and the boat react to the pressure by moving in the direction that offers the least resistance forward. However, as the positive pressure on the face of the sail decreases with the angle of the sail to the wind, a negative, or low pressure, area increases on the back of the sail. This negative pressure, or "suction," is the same force that gives lift to a plane's wing, and, in the case of a well-cut sail, it may account for as much as 80 percent of the force generated to drive the hull through the water when going to windward.

The decrease in pressure on the leeward side of the sail is caused by the difference in the velocity of the airflow over the two sides of the sail. The airflow over the cambered surface is accelerated by being forced to travel farther in the same period of time as the flow across the windward side, and it is a phenomenon of motion that pressure decreases as the velocity of a gas or a fluid is increased.

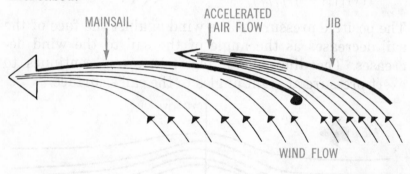

The addition of a jib increases not only the sail area but also the velocity of the airflow across the leeward side of the sail.

Sails are cut for different wind conditions. A pronounced camber (curve in the forward section) will develop more drive in light going but may overpower the boat in a blow. Some sailing rigs can be adjusted to decrease the sail area or flatten the sail, but where strong wind conditions prevail, a sail specially cut for heavy weather is recommended. (See section on heavy weather sailing.)

Sail Plan

When a naval architect designs a hull for a particular purpose, he also develops a sail plan for the craft and establishes how the total sail area will be distributed in relation to the hull's center of gravity and its center of lateral resistance. The plan may range from a simple one consisting of a single sail for a small boat to one involving a complete suit of a dozen or more for an ocean racer.

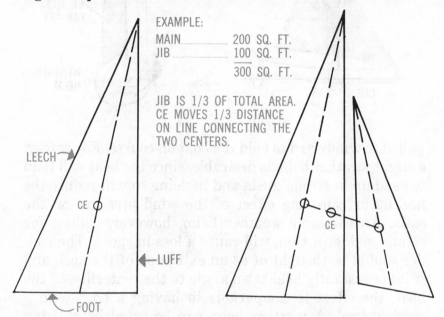

EXAMPLE:

MAIN............ 200 SQ. FT.
JIB .... 100 SQ. FT.
    300 SQ. FT.

JIB IS 1/3 OF TOTAL AREA.
CE MOVES 1/3 DISTANCE
ON LINE CONNECTING THE
TWO CENTERS.

LEECH

CE

CE

←LUFF

FOOT

The center of wind pressure on the sail area can be located, as in the case of the center of lateral resistance on the hull. The point is referred to as the center of effort (CE), and in a jib-headed sail it is approximately one-third the distance up on a line drawn from midpoint on the foot to the peak. A common CE for two or more sails can also be plotted by determining the percentage of total sail area in each sail.

For proper balance, the CE must be at or near a point in a transverse plane directly above the CLR while the boat is sailing across *(reaching)* or into the wind *(beating)*. Otherwise, the boat will have a strong tendency to *head up* into the wind when the CE is behind, or aft of, the CLR, or it will *fall off* (away from the wind direction) if the CE is too far forward. In the first condition the boat is said to have a *weather helm*, because the helm must be

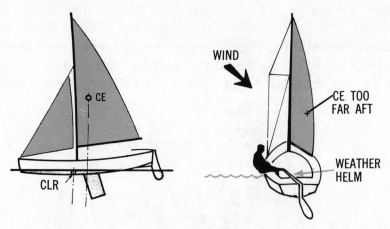

pulled to windward to hold the boat on course. For safety, a slight weather helm is desirable, since the boat will tend to head up in strong gusts and in doing so will reduce the heeling or capsizing effect of the wind pressure on the sails. An excessive weather helm, however, calling for strong rudder action, will cause a loss in speed. The rudder should be thought of as an extension of the keel, and if it is constantly held at an angle to the centerline of the boat, the effect is comparable to having a boat with a crooked keel. A weather helm can be eased by shifting crew or ballast weight aft, by raising the board slightly, or by easing off on the mainsail. The mast may have to be stepped farther forward in extreme cases. When both forces (CE & CLR) are properly balanced, the slight weather helm can be controlled with the fingertips.

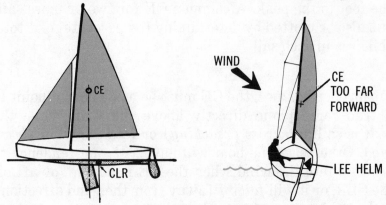

When a boat is sailing on the wind, a lee helm results if

the CE is forward of the CLR, and the condition should be corrected or eliminated as soon as possible. Not only is there a danger of capsizing in sudden puffs as the bow falls off (away from the wind) but there is also the exhausting physical strain involved in pushing the tiller down and away from the helmsman's counterbalancing or hiking position on the high windward side of the boat. To ease a lee helm, shift weight toward the bow or lower the board on a centerboard boat. Also, the mainsail may be hauled in and the jib sheets eased if headsails are carried. The mast may have to be moved farther aft to effect a permanent cure. (NOTE. The naval architect places the CE slightly ahead of the CLR when he designs a sailboat, but because of a shift forward of the CLR caused by the bow wave on the leeward side when under way, a lee helm is avoided.)

Sailing Rigs

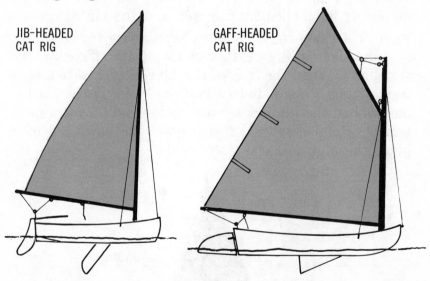

JIB-HEADED
CAT RIG

GAFF-HEADED
CAT RIG

Sailboats are classified or recognized by the shape and number of working sails and by the number and locations of the masts. The various combinations are referred to as *rigs*. The simplest rig is the *cat rig*, consisting of a single sail with the *luff* attached to a mast stepped well forward. Modern cat rigs carry jib-headed mainsails, but in some areas an occasional gaff-headed rig is encountered. The cat rig derives its name from the sail plan of the once popular beamy, centerboard Cape Cod catboat.

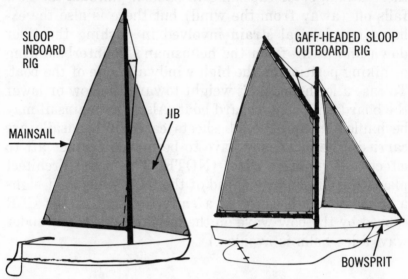

SLOOP
INBOARD
RIG

MAINSAIL

JIB

GAFF-HEADED SLOOP
OUTBOARD RIG

BOWSPRIT

When a jib is added to the sail plan, the mast (and the mainsail) is stepped farther aft, and the rig becomes a sloop. The sloop rig is the most popular rig for small and medium-size sailing craft because of its efficiency and simplicity. When the tack of the jib is attached to a *stem head* fitting it is said to be an *inboard* (sloop) rig. Earlier models had the jib tack secured to the end of a *bowsprit*, which extended several feet beyond the bow, and most often the mainsail was gaff-headed.

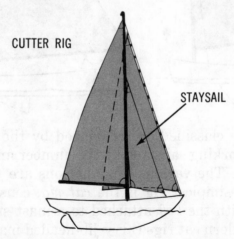

CUTTER RIG

STAYSAIL

The modern cutter rig differs from the sloop in that the cutter generally carries *two working headsails*. The mast is stepped more nearly amidship—at least two-fifths of the deck length aft of the bow—to accommodate a *staysail* between main and jib.

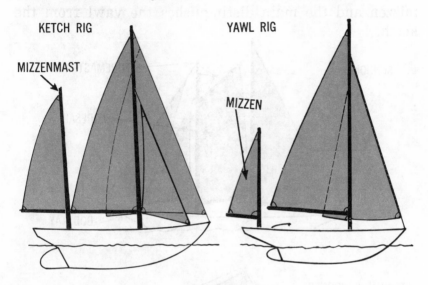

KETCH RIG

MIZZENMAST

YAWL RIG

MIZZEN

On cruising and large ocean racing craft, the sail area is often broken down into several sails, which are carried by two masts.

In comparison with a sloop rig of comparable size, the *divided rig* arrangement provides for smaller sails that are easier to handle, producing less heeling effect with the lower center of effort and affording an opportunity to reduce sail area in bad weather without loss of balance, by lowering selected sails.

The divided rigs of most pleasure craft are either ketch, yawl, or schooner rigs.

The ketch has a *mizzen* mast, somewhat shorter than the main, stepped forward of the rudder post. The working sails generally take the name of the mast or stay to which they are attached, and ketches usually carry a (fore) staysail as well as a jib, main, and mizzen.

Note that the mizzenmast on the yawl is much shorter and

the mizzen sail is smaller than on a ketch of comparable size. Also, on a yawl the mast is stepped aft of the rudder post or the waterline length of the boat. On craft with outboard rudders attached to the transom, or to the stem of double-enders, the marked difference in sail size of the mizzen and the main distinguishes the yawl from the ketch.

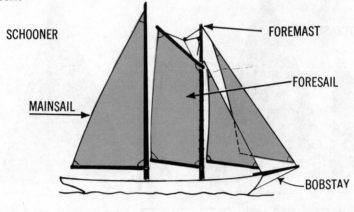

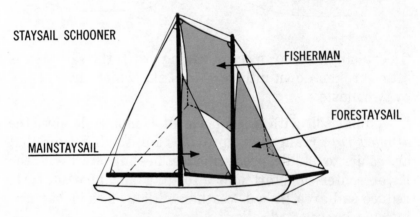

The typical schooner has a *foremast* stepped forward of its taller mainmast. The mainsail is most often jib-headed, but gaffed foresails are also common.

The staysail schooner carries a mainstaysail instead of a foresail between the masts. A fisherman staysail can then be added above the mainstaysail to increase the sail area between the masts. The forestaysail and the mainstaysail are usually interchangeable to avoid confusion in sail handling.

RIGGING

The wires, ropes, and fittings aboard most sailboats are elements of two separate but coordinated rigging systems. One, the *standing rigging*, supports the mast, holds it straight, and also provides means for attaching certain sails. The other system, referred to as the *running rigging*, is used to hoist and trim the sails. Small lateen-rigged craft and some catboats have no standing rigging but depend on the strength of the mast to carry the sail.

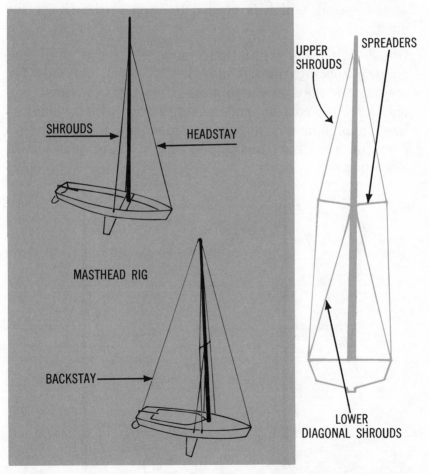

Shrouds and *stays* make up the standing rigging. The shrouds support the mast from the sides and the stays from the end. In the simpler rigs, however, the shrouds also give fore and aft as well as athwartship support to the mast.

Standing rigging has been greatly simplified in recent years. The most popular is the modern *masthead* rig, which consists of a head stay and backstay secured to the top of the mast and a set of upper and lower shrouds. This rig is easier to tune and offers less wind resistance than earlier designs but is more likely to collapse completely should a single fitting give way. The *spreaders*, which the upper shrouds lead over, thrust against the mast when sailing on the wind and prevent it from "bowing" or buckling. They also provide for a more favorable angle of pull, which is needed to support the tip of the mast.

One-design class regulations tend to "freeze" hull and rigging specifications, consequently, older methods for staying the mast are seen more often than the masthead rig. Also, the cost of modernizing a rig, which would at least involve new headsails, discourages a major change-over for what may amount to only a slight increase in efficiency.

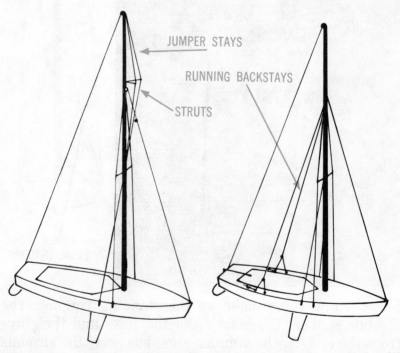

JUMPER STAYS

RUNNING BACKSTAYS

STRUTS

The head stay (to which the jib is attached) and the jib halyard block of many rigging designs are secured several feet below the tip, or *truck*, of the mast. *Jumper stays* leading over *struts* span the area to prevent the mast from bending under the pull of the head stay and the jib. The head, back, and jumper stays are tightly tuned to keep the luff of the jib as straight as possible when on the wind. Too much tension, however, on the head and back stays is likely to compress and bend the mast and may also damage the hull. When the mast is rigged with jumper stays, the lower diagonal shrouds also resist the pull of the jib. They must be tight enough to prevent a bend in the mast at the point where the jumpers are attached.

Running backstays are used in some designs to help resist the pull of the jib. The windward one is set up and the leeward released with each change in tack.

The following tips may be useful in setting up and tuning the standing rigging of small sailing craft:

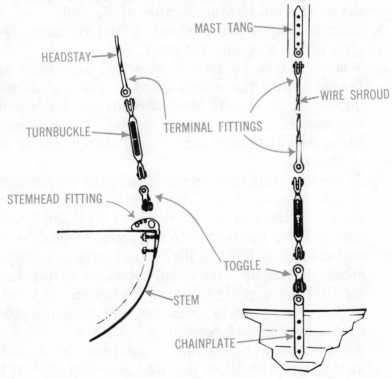

1. Make certain *chainplates*, *mast tangs*, and stem

head fittings are firmly secured. Use bolts instead of screws where possible.

2. Insert toggles between turnbuckles and hull fittings. Metal failure in the eye of the chainplates or the jaws of the turnbuckle may occur unless the connection is made flexible.

3. Check for cracks in fittings that may be *swaged* onto the ends of stainless steel shrouds and stays.

TIGHTEN JUMPERS TO PREVENT MAST FROM BENDING WHEN
WEIGHT EQUAL TO PULL OF THE HEADSTAY AND JIB IS APPLIED HERE.

JUMPER STAYS

4. Adjust the tension of the jumper stays when they are part of the standing rigging before stepping the mast. Stays should be taut enough to prevent the mast from bowing because of jib pull.

5. Attach all appropriate standing and running rigging before stepping the mast.

6. When possible, adjust the *rake* and alignment of the mast while the boat is afloat in water of standing depth. Start with slack shrouds and stays and the mast in a near-vertical position. There should be no weight aboard that might disturb the trim of the boat.

7. Determine from the designer's sail plan the amount of rake needed, if any. Attach a plumb bob to the main halyard and adjust the head stay and backstay to bring the mast into the recommended fore-and-aft inclination. If a jib is to be carried, the stays should be set up with enough tension to prevent the jib from sagging to leeward when on the wind. Sight up the mast to check for compression bends caused by too much tension on the stays.

8. Adjust the lower diagonals, if jumpers are carried, at the same time that the head stay and backstay are tightened.

9. Use the main halyard to check the athwartship

alignment. Hold the tip of the plumb bob at one corner of the transom with the hauling end of the *halyard* secured. Swing the plumb bob to the opposite corner and adjust the upper shrouds until the mast peak is equidistant from each corner. Upper shrouds are generally set tighter than the lowers, but not as tight as the stays.

10. Sight up the mast while the boat is under way. It should be straight in its track and leeward shrouds slack when on the wind. Check the rig from shore or other vantage point as another person sails the boat on and off the wind on different tacks. Remember, do not tighten the standing rigging more than necessary. Otherwise, hull damage may result. *Do not* attempt to correct mast curvature while under way.

11. Lock the turnbuckles so that they will not unscrew under tension. The strands of wire rope have a tendency to untwist when under a load and may cause the top section to back out of the barrel of the turnbuckle.

12. After a final tuning of the standing rigging, pack the barrels of the turnbuckles with waterproof grease and wrap the exposed threads and barrel with waterproof adhesive.

Running Rigging

The lines that are hauled on in handling sails make up the *running rigging* of a sailboat.

Cat rigs have a simple system consisting of a *halyard* to hoist the sail and a *sheet* to control it. Additional sheets and halyards are added when the sail plans are enlarged, each designated by the name of the sail to which it is attached. They are led, or *rove*, through *blocks* or *fairleaders*, over masthead *sheaves*, and sometimes around winches for convenience and to increase their *purchasing*, or holding, power.

Running rigging also includes *topping lifts, clew out-*

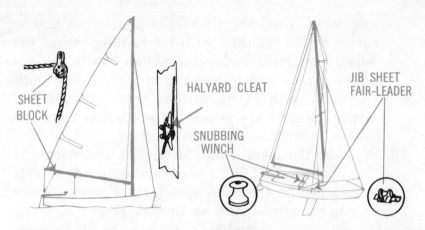

SHEET BLOCK

HALYARD CLEAT

SNUBBING WINCH

JIB SHEET FAIR-LEADER

hauls, and *downhauls* when they are part of the rigging plan. Instead of a topping lift to support the weight of the boom when the sail is lowered, a short *lanyard*, or *pendant*, lashed to the permanent backstay could be substituted. Small sailing craft, however, most often use a *boom crutch* or the main halyard.

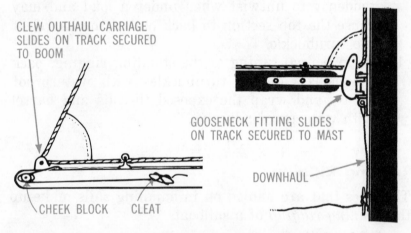

CLEW OUTHAUL CARRIAGE SLIDES ON TRACK SECURED TO BOOM

GOOSENECK FITTING SLIDES ON TRACK SECURED TO MAST

DOWNHAUL

CHEEK BLOCK   CLEAT

The *clew outhaul*, as the name implies, is used to haul out and adjust the tension of the foot of the sail along the boom, and the *downhaul* regulates the tension of the luff.

Halyards and sheets for small sailing craft are usually made of 1/4- or 5/16-inch manila or dacron rope, but many racing classes have a section of stainless steel wire in the halyard that carries the load when the sail is fully raised. Wire has less stretch than rope and offers less wind resistance, but a rope tail is needed for handling and cleating purposes. Generally, a ratchet winch is used to raise the last few inches of sail and to apply the desired tension.

Sheets serve two important functions. First, they adjust the angle of the sail in relation to wind direction, and second, when on the wind, they must exert a downward pull on the leech of the sail in order to preserve its airfoil or winglike shape.

The main boom sheet is usually *rove* through a *traveler* and block arrangement between the end of the boom and the stern or the transom of the boat. The choice of combinations is based on the sail area and the purchase power needed to control the sail.

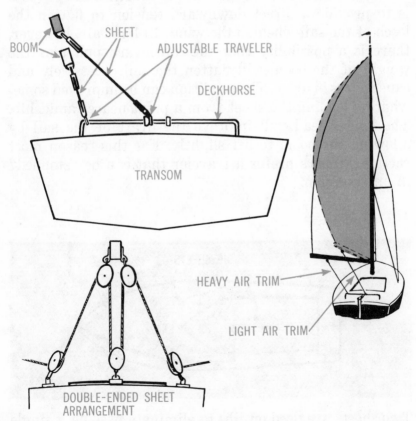

The traveler may be a ring, slide, or some other fitting to which a sheet block is attached. It slides from one quarter of the transom to the other on a *deck horse* or

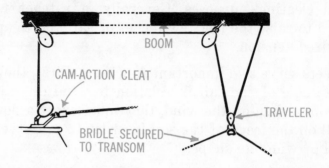

bridle with each change in tack. Steel rods are generally rigged as deck horses on larger sailing craft, but smaller boats usually have a track and slide or a slack stainless steel wire arrangement. Collectively, the combination of fittings is referred to as the *traveler* and its main purpose is to provide a direct downward tension to flatten the leech of the sail when on the wind. In light air, however, there is a possibility that the downward pull plus the weight of the boom will flatten the sail excessively and cause a loss in drive. The condition can be improved somewhat by leading the sheet from a point nearer amidship. The longer lead will improve the draft of the sail by allowing the boom to lift slightly. For this reason most racing skippers prefer a traveler that can be "stopped" in any position.

Jib Sheets

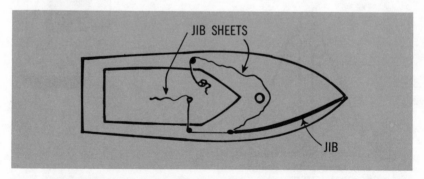

Two sheets are used on jibs to eliminate passing a single sheet from side to side around the mast with each change in tack. They are often fastened to the clew of the jib by detachable fittings, but on the smaller sails, in order to

34

save weight, the sheets are usually spliced on, or a long line is secured at its center by a clove hitch to the clew cringle to form the two sheets. Note that the sheets are long enough to lead, without tension, from the clew and around the mast into the cockpit.

The angle of pull, or *lead*, of the jib sheet is all-important if the jib is to be trimmed properly, especially when on the wind. The sheet not only must apply equal tension to two unequal sides of the triangular sail but must also direct the angle of the accelerated airflow through the "slot" across the back of the mainsail.

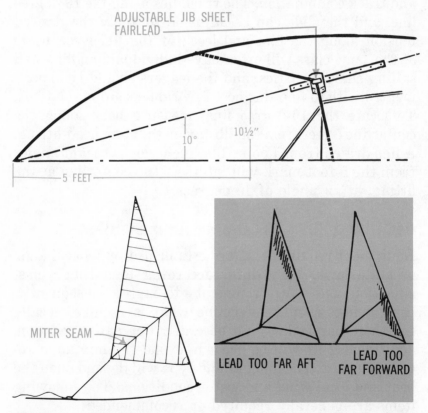

ADJUSTABLE JIB SHEET FAIRLEAD

10° 10½"

5 FEET

MITER SEAM

LEAD TOO FAR AFT   LEAD TOO FAR FORWARD

The key to jib efficiency is in the location of the jib sheet fair-leader. Experience indicates that the directional airflow through the slot can be regulated most effectively when the fair-leader lies on a line running at a 10-degree angle from the stem, or tack, of the jib. The fore-and-aft position of the lead which determines the tension on the leech and the foot of the jib, is located slightly forward of an extension of the *miter* line where it intercepts the 10-degree line. The fore-and-aft location of the leader should be adjusted so that the luff of the jib *breaks*, or flutters, evenly throughout its length when the boat is brought up into the wind. Once the location of the fair-leaders have been established, make certain the tack of the jib is always secured the same distance from the stem head fitting.

For more efficient sheet leads on different headings and wind speeds, the fair-leader is often attached to a slide and track combination. The track lies along the 10-degree line, and the slide can be adjusted to apply the desired tension along the foot and leech of the jib. Even boats of the same class will often have individual handling and sailing characteristics, and the leaders should be experimented with to find the most favorable position. (NOTE. To locate the 10-degree line, measure back along the centerline 5 feet from the jibstay or the stem head fitting. A line drawn from a point 10½ inches out at right angles from the 5-foot mark will intersect the centerline at the fitting, at an angle of 10 degrees.)

REQUIRED AND RECOMMENDED EQUIPMENT

Equipment requirements are established by federal and/or state laws. They differ according to a boat's classification and vary from state to state; consequently, boat owners should determine what is required locally for their particular type of craft. For safe operation, additional gear will be needed beyond the minimum required by law. The amount and type will depend upon the boat and local wind and water conditions. The following items are generally required or recommended:

1. A Coast Guard approved lifesaving device for each person aboard. Weak swimmers or nonswimmers should wear one at all times.

2. Paddles or oars. These are often needed to maneuver when sails are lowered or during periods of calm.

Lights Required on Boats Underway Between Sunset and Sunrise
For Power Boats Under 65 Feet and All Sailing Vessels
Vessels at anchor must display anchor lights except those under 65 feet in "special anchorage area"

MOTORBOAT ACT (Act of April 25, 1940).—
used where Inland, Western Rivers and Great Lakes Rules apply

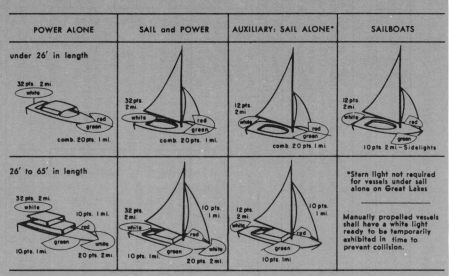

INTERNATIONAL RULES.—
required on high seas, may be used inland

Minimum Federally Required Equipment

EQUIPMENT	CLASS A (Less than 16 feet)	CLASS 1 (16 feet to less than 26 feet)	CLASS 2 (26 feet to less than 40 feet)	CLASS 3 (40 feet to not more than 65 feet)
BACK-FIRE FLAME ARRESTER.	One approved device on each carburetor of all gasoline engines installed after April 25, 1940, except outboard motors.			
VENTILATION	At least two ventilator ducts (at least one exhaust duct installed so as to extend from the open atmosphere to the lower portion of the bilge and at least one intake duct installed so as to extend to a point at least midway to the bilge or at least below the level of the carburetor air intake). These ducts must be fitted with cowls or their equivalent for the purpose of properly and efficiently ventilating the bilges of every engine and fuel tank compartment of boats constructed or decked over after April 25, 1940, using gasoline or other fuel of a flashpoint less than 110 degrees F.			
BELL	None*	None*	One, which when struck produces a clear, bell-like tone of full round characteristics.	
LIFESAVING DEVICES	One approved life preserver, buoyant vest, ring buoy, special purpose water safety buoyant device, or buoyant cushion for each person on board or being towed on water skis.			One approved life preserver or ring buoy for each person on board.
WHISTLE	None*	One hand, mouth, or power operated, audible at least ½ mile.	One hand or power operated, audible at least 1 mile.	One power operated, audible at least 1 mile.
FIRE EXTINGUISHER, PORTABLE — When *no* fixed fire extinguishing system is installed in machinery space.	At least one B-I type approved hand portable fire extinguisher. (Not required on outboard motorboats less than 26 feet in length and not carrying passengers for hire if the construction of such motorboats will not permit the entrapment of explosive or flammable gases or vapors.)		At least two B-I type approved hand portable fire extinguishers; or at least one B-II type approved hand portable fire extinguishers.	At least three B-I type approved hand portable fire extinguishers; or at least one B-I type *plus* one B-II type approved hand portable fire extinguisher.
When fixed fire extinguishing system is installed in machinery space.	None.	None.	At least one B-I type approved hand portable fire extinguisher.	At least two B-I type approved hand portable fire extinguishers; or at least one B-II type approved hand portable fire extinguisher.
	B-I type approved hand portable fire extinguishers contain: foam, 1¼ to 2½ gallons; or carbon dioxide, 4 up to 15 pounds; or dry chemical, 2 up to 10 pounds. B-II type approved hand portable fire extinguishers contain: foam, 2½ gallons; or carbon dioxide, 15 pounds; or dry chemical, 10 up to 20 pounds.			

*Not required by the Motorboat Act of 1940. However, the "Rules of the Road" require these vessels to sound proper signals.

3. Bailer. Water in the bilge decreases stability. Use a sponge, can, or pump.
4. Anchor. A light anchor can be lowered to prevent being carried away by currents, tides, or high winds.
5. Extra line. Small sail craft should have an extra line aboard as well as a bow line permanently secured to the craft.
6. Boathook. Use a boathook to fend off and also to pick up mooring lines.

Lightweight outboard motors are not only useful during periods of calm but also can be a means of quickly reaching a point of safety when bad weather threatens. It should be remembered, however, that a sailboat's classification changes to that of a motorboat while under power, and regulations involving rights of way, lights, fire extinguishers, and ventilation of enclosed areas will apply. *(See the American Red Cross booklet* Basic Outboard Boating.)

BOARDING AND RIGGING PROCEDURES

Small boat sailors generally expect, and are prepared for, an occasional capsize, especially when in competition, but most of the serious and painful sailboat mishaps occur in getting on or off the boat while it is tied alongside a pier or secured to a mooring and while rigging and unrigging the boat before and after an outing. Practices, procedures, and progressions for getting under way will differ somewhat, depending on the size and type of boat and how it is moored, but the following steps are considered basic:

1. *Wear nonskid deck shoes and appropriate clothing.* Sailing a small boat calls for agility and coordinated movements on the part of everybody aboard. Not only are slips and falls (within the boat) the major causes of serious sailboat injuries but also the mistiming in shifting weight because of a slip or a fall

can result in a capsize. Avoid clothing that would impede movement or get tangled or fouled in the running rigging, especially in the blocks. Long, flowing hair should be covered for the same reason. Keep hip pockets empty of combs and bulky handkerchiefs. Also, knife sheaths carried on the hip are likely to catch under the cockpit coaming when it is necessary to shift body weight quickly to the high side.

2. *Check for waves or wakes of passing boats before boarding.* An unexpected lurch of the boat at the moment of boarding can have serious consequences. When alongside a pier, the boat should be secured with bow and stern lines that will prevent it from moving outward appreciably. When boarding at a mooring, hold the tender or shoreboat alongside but a few inches away from the moored craft. *Keep hands off the gunwales* to avoid pinching or smashing the fingers between the two boats. Swing one foot aboard the sailboat while holding onto the edge of its cockpit or coaming, and slowly transfer the body weight from one boat to the other to maintain balance as the boats adjust to their new floating levels. When someone is stepping from a small tender into a light sailing pram, the change in floating levels between the two may range as high as 6 or 7 inches.

3. *Keep weight low and hands clear when boarding.* When the boat is alongside a pier, enter near amidship and step as close to the centerline as possible. If a hand is placed on the coaming or the pier for support, take care that the fingers are not pinched between the boat and the pier. Place sailbags and other equipment along the edge of the pier when entering the boat and transfer them aboard afterwards.

4. *Lower the centerboard,* unless the boat has a fixed keel. The motion of the boat while being made ready for sail will be reduced somewhat with the board

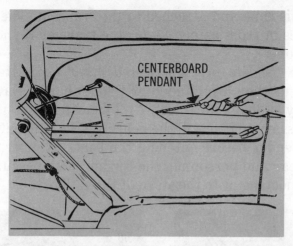

CENTERBOARD
PENDANT

down. At a mooring, however, when there is a stiff breeze blowing, the boat is likely to *yaw*, or "sail" back and forth, if the board is lowered. Boats will react differently, and individual characteristics must be learned by testing and experimenting.

5. *Bail out the boat.* Water in the bilges increases the danger of slipping on wet surfaces, and the extra weight when heeled over seriously effects trim and stability as well as response to wind, wave, and rudder action.

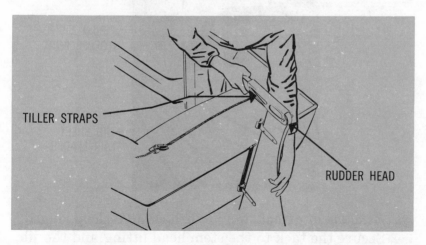

TILLER STRAPS

RUDDER HEAD

6. *Ship, or attach, the rudder and the tiller.* The rudder assembly for small boats is normally stowed aboard under the bow deck or a seat but if taken ashore with other gear it should be brought aboard

at this time and attached to the transom. The tiller comes in from astern *under* the traveler if the boat has one.

7. *Stow the life preservers and other gear,* item by item as they are handed or taken aboard. Save the bulky sailbags until last. At a mooring, it is usually necessary to place all the gear into the sailboat from the tender before entering the boat. After transfer of gear and personnel, the tender can be secured to the mooring or to the stern of the sailboat.

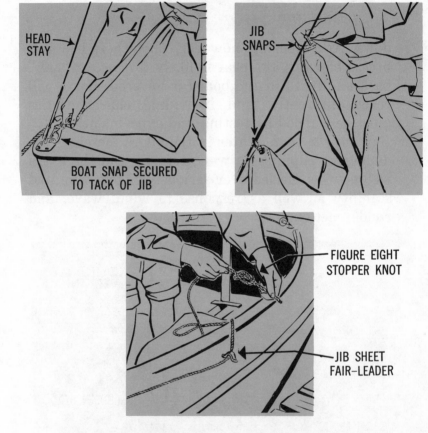

8. *Bend on, or attach, the jib* if the boat is sloop rigged. Secure the tack to the stem head fitting and the jib snaps or slides, starting from the bottom, to the head stay. Check each snap carefully as it is slipped onto the stay to see it is not twisted. Clear the jib halyard but leave the hauling end attached to its

cleat. (The jib halyard is usually rigged to the port side of the mast.) Check aloft to be sure the halyard is not wrapped around a stay and then secure it to the peak of the jib. Rope halyards can be attached with a figure eight knot. Straighten out the foot of the jib and lead the jib sheets back through the fairleaders into the cockpit. Tie a figure eight stopper knot to prevent the sheets from accidentally coming adrift. Do not raise the jib at this time. (NOTE. On small sailing craft, attach the jib if possible without going forward of the mast. Too much weight in the bow while stepping around the mast is likely to cause a capsize.)

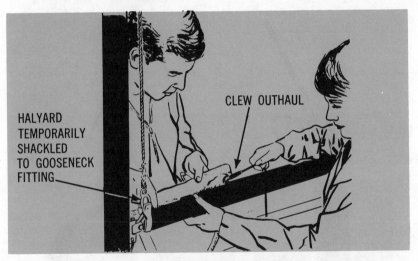

HALYARD TEMPORARILY SHACKLED TO GOOSENECK FITTING

CLEW OUTHAUL

9. *Bend on the mainsail.* Start with the clew and slip the slides onto the boom track working from the clew towards the tack. If the boom is slotted, pull the outhaul to the end of the boom as a crew member "feeds" the bolt rope into the slot. Secure the tack to the gooseneck fitting and adjust the tension of the sail along the foot by hauling on and securing the clew outhaul. (A second short line, called an *earing*, should be passed through the clew cringle and tied snugly around the boom. The weight of the boom and the downward pull of the mainsheet would otherwise subject the aftermost slides and/or

the bolt rope to excessive strain.) The tension along the foot should be adjusted according to sailing condition—little or none for light air to an amount approximating the tension exerted on the leech when the sail is trimmed for beating to windward in heavy going. Insert the *battens* before attaching the halyard to the headboard if the mast is slotted; otherwise, the halyard can be secured and the slides slipped onto the mast track before the battens are put in their pockets. In either case, before hoisting or attaching the sail to the mast, start at the tack and check the length of the luff to be sure it is not twisted.

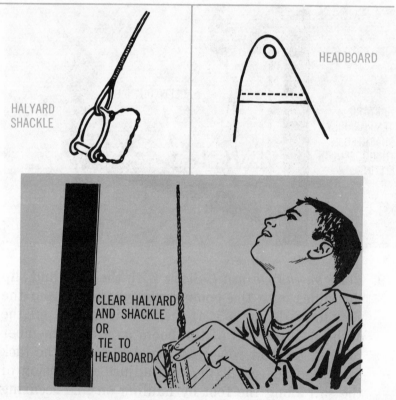

10. *Shackle the halyard to the headboard.* Be sure the halyard is clear of stays or spreaders. Wire halyards are usually fitted with shackles but rope ones may be secured with a figure eight knot.
11. *Clear the mainsheet.* The sheet must be free to run

through the blocks as the sail is raised. The coiled sheet is usually laid flat on the floor of the cockpit with the part leading to the boom coming from the *top* of the coil.

12. *Check the wind direction.* The boat should be headed into the wind before you attempt to hoist the sails. When the boat is alongside a pier, release the stern line or move the boat to the leeward side of the pier so that it can "weathervane" into the wind. Auxiliary sailboats usually leave a pier under power and the sails are hoisted when clear, with the boat held into the wind by the motor.

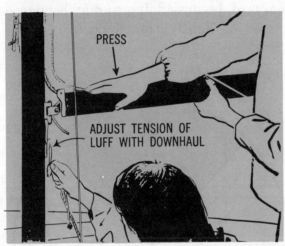

13. *Raise the mainsail.* The weight of the boom is usually carried by a *topping lift* or a *boom crutch* until the sail is fully hoisted. On small boats, however, it is a common practice to use the main halyard as a topping lift while the boat is at its mooring. In this instance, to avoid stretching the leech of the sail, have the boom held by a crew member while the sail is being raised. Look aloft while hauling on the halyard to see that the battens do not become fouled under a spreader. The tension of the luff, as in the case of the foot of the sail, should be adjusted according to wind conditions. Use the downhaul to regulate the tension after the sail has been fully raised; or if the gooseneck fitting is permanently

attached to the mast, sway on the main halyard to tighten the luff. Cleat the halyard and coil and hang it to the cleat *before* proceeding to the next step.

14. *Hoist the jib* if the craft is sloop rigged. The luff of the jib must be tight if the boat is to sail efficiently to windward. For this reason a nonstretch wire instead of a rope is sewn into the luff to carry the strain. Rope halyards will stretch after the boat has been sailed awhile, and the slack will have to be removed by again swaying on the jib halyard. (NOTE. Do not apply too much tension on the jib halyard, because doing so may bend or compress the mast of lightly rigged boats.)

POINTS OF SAILING

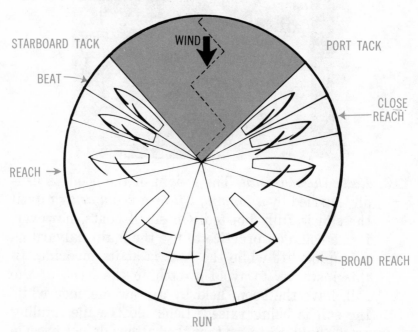

Points of sailing, sometimes called sailing positions, relate to the angle between a sailboat's heading, or course, and the direction of the wind. The headings are broadly defined as *beating* (on the wind), *reaching* (across the wind), and *running* (off the wind).

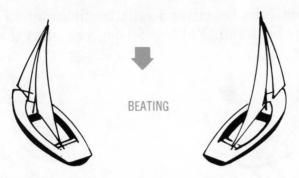

BEATING

When on a beat, a boat is sailing as close to the eye of the wind as possible, about 45 degrees. The mainsail is sheeted in, with the end of the boom over the corner of or slightly inside the transom, depending on the cut of the sail and the strength of the wind. Sails must be kept full to maintain maximum speed. If the boat is pointed too high into the wind, or *pinched,* the forward part of the sail will start to *luff,* or flutter, and cause a loss in drive and speed. Progress directly to windward is made by *tacking,* or changing the boat's heading from one side (of the wind) to the other. The boat is said to be *close-hauled* on the port tack when the wind is coming from the left and it is close-hauled on the *starboard* tack when beating with the wind on the right.

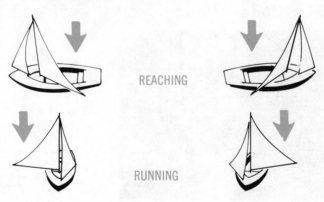

REACHING

RUNNING

The boat is on a *reach* when the wind is *abeam,* or at a 90-degree, angle to the heading and the boat is *running,* or sailing before the wind, when the wind is blowing from astern. Note that when the boat is reaching, the sheet is eased until the boom (and sail) is out about 45 degrees from the boat and at almost 90 degrees when the boat is running.

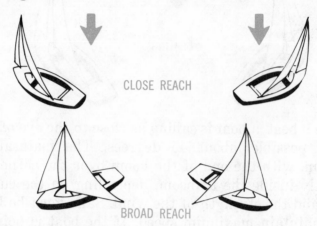

CLOSE REACH

BROAD REACH

Close reach and *broad* reach are intermediate points of sailing between a beat and a reach and between a reach and a run. Obviously, the boat can sail at any angle between a beat and a run, but the heading takes its name from the nearest major or intermediate point. The sails must be trimmed accordingly with each change in heading or wind direction.

Getting Under Way

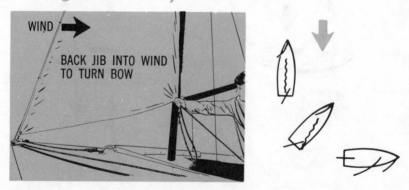

WIND

BACK JIB INTO WIND
TO TURN BOW

With the sails up and luffing, or flying free, the boat will be pointing into the wind at its mooring unless a strong tide or current is adversely affecting the hull. Before casting off the mooring or bow line, decide upon the course and determine if the boat will be on a starboard or a port tack. Sit forward of the end of the tiller and slightly to the side that the wind will be coming from when under way. Crew, if any, should also be placed as near the amidship section as possible to avoid trimming

the boat down by the bow. To get under way, cast off the mooring line and hold the tiller dead center as the boat drifts back stern first. Push the tiller away at about a 45-degree angle, and the rudder will turn the stern and swing the boat broadside to the wind. Haul in on the mainsheet until the sails fill, or stop luffing, and bring the tiller back to the center position as the boat begins to move forward. With a sloop rig the jib can be *backed* into the wind by a crewman to help force the bow around as it drifts back on the rudder. The crewmen would then haul in on the leeward jib sheet and see that the windward sheet is clear while the helmsman trims the mainsheet and tends the tiller. Take a turn around a cleat with the mainsheet to decrease the strain of a direct pull but *do not* secure it. The sheet on small boats is held in the hand —not wrapped around it—so that it can be eased instantly when necessary. The jib sheet is usually wrapped around a snubbing winch two or three times and is tended by a crewman.

Reaching

Reaching, or sailing back and forth at right angles across the face of the wind, should be practiced first by the

REACHING

beginner. It is the most pleasant way to sail and also the fastest and easiest, but it is important to have a definite objective to steer for and not just sail back and forth aimlessly if sailing skills are to be learned quickly. When the boat is on a course more or less at right angles to the wind, the boom will be out at approximately 45 degrees. To trim the sail correctly, keep the boat on course, or heading for its objective, and slowly ease the mainsheet until the luff of the sail begins to flutter a few inches away from the mast. With the boat still held on course, haul in on the sheet until the flutter stops, or the "canvas goes to sleep." Next, trim the jib in the same manner if one is carried.

Develop a constant awareness of the wind and its direction as early as possible. A 6- or 8-inch length of yarn or ribbon tied to the shrouds or a *telltale* at the top of the mast will help show the wind direction, but a more accurate indicator, especially in light air, is one's own sense of touch and hearing. The airflow can be felt on the cheek or the back of the neck and it can usually be "tuned in" by turning the head slowly from side to side until both ears record the same pitch.

Developing sensitivity to wind direction is the most essential element in learning to sail and usually it is the slowest for the beginner to master.

Adjusting the Centerboard

To reduce unnecessary surface friction while underway, "trim" the centerboard or daggerboard as carefully as the sails. It is seldom necessary to lower the board all the way down in a well-designed boat even while beating to windward. To do so may weaken the centerboard well, since considerable leverage is exerted by a fully lowered board. Lowering the board three-fourths of the way is generally sufficient even when sailing close-hauled, and of course it can be raised completely while running.

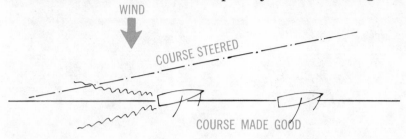

To adjust the board while on a reach, hold the boat on course and raise the board slowly until the boat begins to slip sideways, or make leeway. Check the wake. When the centerline of the boat is at a marked angle to the wake, the boat is making leeway. Lower the board until the boat can be held on course and nearly in line with the wake. A slight amount of leeway can be expected while reaching or beating in any sailboat, and the heading should be slightly upwind of the objective to allow for the drift. The amount of the change in course would depend upon how much is needed to keep the boat moving in a straight line over the bottom, although slightly sideways, towards the objective. Establish a "fix" or line up the objective with another landmark and steer the boat to keep the "range closed." The CLR will change slightly with each change in depth of the centerboard, and it may be necessary to shift the crew's weight fore or aft to avoid a lee or an excessive weather helm.

When the boat is on the wind in light air, the drive of the sail can be increased by shifting crew weight to leeward. The airfoil shape of the sail is improved by its own weight as the boat is heeled. On flat- and V-bottom boats the wetted "surface" area (and resistance) is also reduced by heeling the boat. As the chine digs in and the side of the boat offers lateral resistance, the board may be raised accordingly to further reduce resistance to forward motion.

SHIFT WEIGHT TO
LEEWARD
IN LIGHT AIR

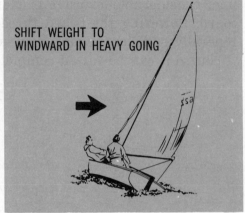

SHIFT WEIGHT TO
WINDWARD IN HEAVY GOING

In fresh to strong winds, counterbalance the heeling effect by shifting the crew weight to windward (hiking). If necessary, ease off on the mainsheet until the sail begins to luff and loses some of its drive. On a sloop, the drive of the mainsail can also be reduced by sheeting the jib in tighter so that the air flow through the slot will *back-wind* the main and distort its effective airfoil shape.

Coming About

To reverse the course and sail back to the point of departure, turn the boat into the wind and bring it around on the opposite tack. To *come about*, or change tack from one reach to another, follow the procedure below:

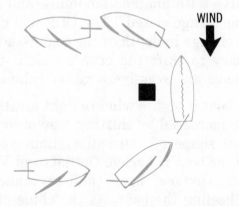

WIND

1. *Have the boat moving as fast as wind and water conditions permit.* As the boat is turned into the

wind, its momentum must carry it around onto the opposite tack. There is generally no problem in boats with heavy keels, but lightweight centerboarders are likely to stall, or go *in irons*, when they are turned directly into the wind unless they have sufficient way on and are quickly brought about.

2. *Warn the crew*, if any, before changing course. At the helmsman's call of "ready about" or "stand by to come about" the crew prepares to handle the sheets and move to the opposite side as the boom crosses overhead. Check for other boats in the vicinity before starting the turn.

3. *Move the tiller "hard alee."* At the command of execution the helmsman pushes the tiller firmly but smoothly to leeward (toward the sail) about 45 degrees. *At the same time,* when coming about from a reach, the sheets must be pulled in to keep the sails full (of wind) and driving, especially the main, as long as possible. Unless the sails are kept full as the boat swings around to the "close-hauled" position, the boat will slow down and probably go in irons. *Keep hands off the boom.* Any attempt to move the sail over to the new tack will only cause it to be back-winded and force the boat back on its former heading. In heavy going, if possible, wait for a lull before coming about.

4. *Trim the sails* for reaching after the course has been reversed and the boat is heading back towards its mooring. (Should the boat stall, bow into the wind, follow the procedure for getting underway from a mooring; that is, move the tiller 45 degrees away from the side that is to be kept to windward and back-wind the jib, if the boat is sloop rigged, as the boat drifts back stern first. Haul in the sheet when the wind is once again coming in from the side and proceed to get under way on course. In very light air the boat may be coaxed around by rudder action (not permitted in racing).

True and Apparent Wind

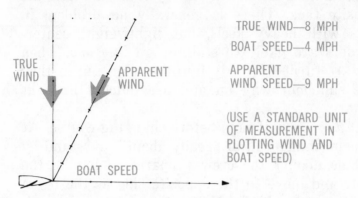

TRUE WIND—8 MPH

BOAT SPEED—4 MPH

APPARENT
WIND SPEED—9 MPH

(USE A STANDARD UNIT
OF MEASUREMENT IN
PLOTTING WIND AND
BOAT SPEED)

When practicing reaching back and forth between two markers that are at right angles to the wind, note that the wind apparently increases in velocity and changes direction as the boat begins to pick up speed after coming about. The effect is caused by the boat's movement through an air mass. The apparent wind experienced in a fast power boat, for example, will be almost directly ahead and equal to the boat's speed through the water, although the true wind remains at a right angle to the boat. This fact accounts for the ability of slow boats to point higher than fast boats. Consequently, when the boat is sailing on any heading except before the wind, sail trimming is based on the apparent wind, the direction of which is indicated by the telltales and other signs of air flow aboard the boat. The wind *veers* when it changes direction from left to right, or clockwise, and it *backs* in the opposite direction. When the boat is sailing on a predetermined course, however, the wind is said to *haul* when it moves toward the bow or *heads* the boat and it veers when the direction changes toward the stern.

Close and Broad Reaching

The next logical step in the progression of learning how to handle a boat is practice in sailing slightly on and off the wind. Again, this sailing should be done between two marks or definite objectives. To proceed from a reach to a close reach, haul in the main boom midway to the corner of the transom from its reaching position and at the same time keep a restraining hand on the tiller to prevent the boat from swinging too far into the wind or, perhaps, from coming about, since drawing in the sail will increase the weather helm, and there will be a tendency for the boat to turn into the wind. Allow the boat to head into the wind just far enough to produce a slight luff next to the mast. As in reaching, hold the boat on course and trim the main to the point where the flutter just disappears. Note that it is not unusual for wind directions to fluctuate, especially in light air, and it may be necessary to change course slightly to keep the sails properly trimmed. An increase in wind velocity will also change the direction of the apparent wind to nearer that of the true wind. When steering for a definite objective, however, hold the boat on course and trim the sails to accommodate changes in apparent wind direction.

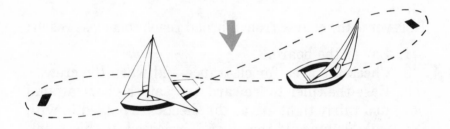

To reverse the course from a close to a broad reach, it may not be necessary to haul in the main sheet and to keep the sail full to bring the boat about but it is a good practice to do so. Speed drops quickly, especially in lightweight centerboarders, as soon as the sails begin to luff, and further time is lost after the boat comes about unless the sails are quickly filled.

As in coming about from a reach, push the tiller to leeward about 45 degrees and haul in the sheet to keep the mainsail driving as long as possible. (A properly trimmed jib for a close reach need not be hauled in when coming about. Hauling it in may slow down or stop the turning maneuver; however, the weather sheet must be released *after* the bow passes the eye of the wind, and the leeward sheet must be taken in.) Hold the tiller over until the 180-degree turn is completed and at the same time ease off on the main sheet as the sail fills. The boom should be at approximately right angles to the wind while the boat is on a broad reach or a run, but the exact angle will vary with the cut of the sail and can only be determined by experimenting. The board may be partially or completely raised, depending on the type of hull. A flat- or round-bottom boat will need more board than a vee-bottom craft with hard chines and vertical sides.

Note that the wind velocity will appear to drop as the boat gets under way *off* the wind. The speed of the apparent wind will be that of the true wind minus the downwind speed of the boat. Avoid trimming the boat "down by the bow" but keep the lower part of the transom above the waterline, if possible, to avoid drag by moving the crew weight slightly forward.

To reverse the course from a broad reach to a close reach:

1. Lower the board.
2. Check the area for clearance and warn the crew.
3. Ease the tiller to leeward and sail the boat around in a fairly tight arc as the sheets are hauled in with sails driving. If the tiller is released at this point, the boat is likely to spin around and stall. Keep the main driving as long as possible as the boat is brought about on the other tack.
4. Bring the tiller back to center after coming about to stop the boat from *falling off* beyond a close reach position.
5. Trim the sails as before for a close reach.

If the boat is sloop rigged, the jib should be hauled in along with the main up to a close reach position when coming about from a reach or off the wind. Otherwise, the unnecessary windage caused by the flapping sail will slow down the boat in the turn and may cause it to go *in irons*.

Sailing close and broad reaches should be practiced on

both tacks. To change from one close reach to another, haul in the main as the tiller is put to leeward. After the boat swings over on the opposite tack, bring the tiller back toward center to prevent the boat from continuing the turn and ease the sheet slightly as the close-hauled main begins to fill. The board need not be changed when the boat goes from one close reach to another. The jib sheets are switched as the boat comes about but are not hauled in as part of the maneuver.

Beating, Tacking and Running

Practice in sailing to windward and before the wind can be conveniently combined during the learning phase. Short beats followed by runs back to the mooring area will provide an opportunity to develop boating handling skills without going far afield.

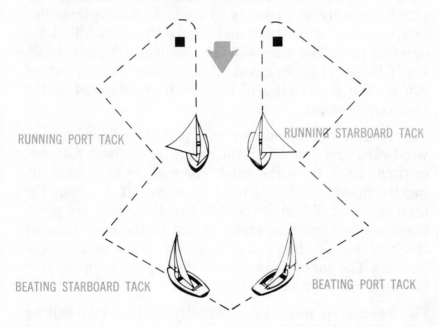

RUNNING PORT TACK   RUNNING STARBOARD TACK

BEATING STARBOARD TACK   BEATING PORT TACK

A sailboat beats to windward by sailing *close-hauled* first on one tack and then on the other. The sheets are hauled in with the end of the boom over the corner of the transom or nearly amidship, depending on the cut of the sails and hull design, but sails must be full and the boat kept moving at near maximum speed. If the boat is *pinched* after the sails have been trimmed, speed will drop and the craft may stall. When the boat is sailing close-hauled, the mark or objective is usually upwind of the course and the *boat* is steered to keep the sails driving at peak efficiency; whereas, in other points of sailing the boat is held on course and it is the *sails* that are trimmed with each wind shift.

The board is kept down while beating, since the tendency to make leeway is greatest when the boat is sailing close-hauled, and the crew should be kept as low as possible to reduce windage.

To change tack from one close-hauled position to the other, simply push the tiller to leeward about 45 degrees and return it to near center as soon as the boat has passed the eye of the wind. The maneuver should be executed smoothly and quickly to avoid an appreciable loss in speed during the turn and before the sails fill on the opposite tack. The main will trim itself for the new heading if the sheet is not eased off or allowed to run, but, of course, the jib sheets will have to be readjusted as the boat comes about.

To change from a beat to a run, pull the tiller slowly to windward and ease off on the sheets as the boat *falls off*, or turns away from the wind. The main is kept full during the maneuver but it must be eased off at about the turning speed. When the boat is directly before the wind, the boom is almost at right angles to the centerline of the boat but it should not touch or chafe against the shrouds. The board can be raised during the turn or after the turn has been completed.

The helmsman must be constantly alert when sailing before the wind. Wind shifts are likely to go unnoticed with the drop in velocity of the apparent wind and if there is a *following sea*, wave action may lift the stern and partially bury the bow, causing the boat to *yaw*.

An accidental jibe is the chief danger when running. A jibe occurs when a yaw or a wind shift allows the wind to get behind the leech of the sail and causes it to swing violently over on the opposite tack through an arc of nearly 180 degrees. During the jibe, there is danger of being struck by the boom as it passes over the cockpit and there is always the possibility of losing the mast or capsizing. A jibe under controlled conditions is a proper maneuver, which will be discussed later, but an accidental jibe must be guarded against, especially in running before strong winds.

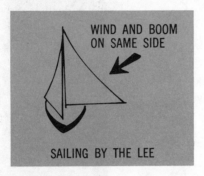

Sailing *by the lee* is the main cause of accidental jibes. The condition exists in a situation when the wind is coming in from the same side of the boat that the boom is on.

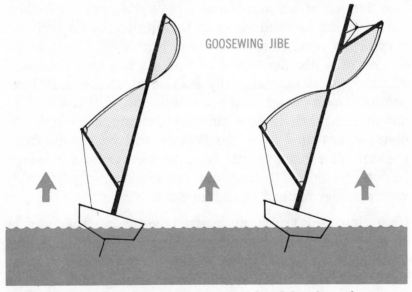

A slight yaw or change in course in this situation may allow the wind to get behind the sail and cause it to jibe.

An accidental *goosewing* jibe occurs when the boom lifts and wildly swings over with only the lower part of the sail. The goosewing jibe is more likely to occur with gaff-headed sails, but jib-headed sails are not immune. The lower part of the main (and boom) is intentionally jibed back to correct the condition.

Tacking Downwind

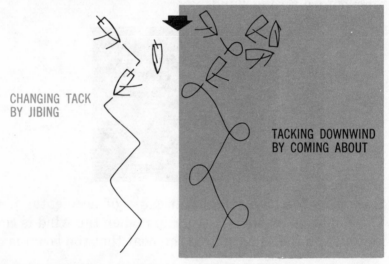

CHANGING TACK
BY JIBING

TACKING DOWNWIND
BY COMING ABOUT

The danger of an accidental jibe while running before the wind can be minimized by tacking back and forth on very broad reaches toward the objective. Not only is the danger of a jibe decreased by tacking but also the speed of the boat is substantially increased. Some craft, depending upon design and sea conditions, will reach their downwind mark in less time by tacking, although the distance traveled over the bottom will be considerably greater. The fastest route for a particular boat can only be determined by testing and experimenting, preferably with another boat of the same class.

Changing tack from one broad reach to another can be done by coming about or by making an intentional jibe. Coming about is the slower maneuver but should be practiced first since it is similar to changing tack from a broad to a close reach. After heading up into the wind and changing over on the opposite tack, simply keep the tiller over and ease off on the sheets as the sails fill until the boat is once again on a very broad reach. The board may have to be lowered in order to come about, then can be raised again after the turn has been completed.

The Intentional Jibe

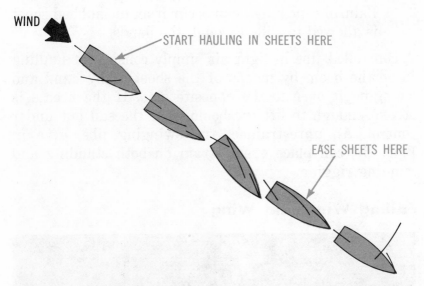

WIND

START HAULING IN SHEETS HERE

EASE SHEETS HERE

The intentional jibe is the quickest and most efficient means of changing tack when sailing off the wind but it is essential, especially in heavy weather, to maintain rigid control of the boat and sails during the maneuver. To jibe while running or to jibe from one broad reach to the other:

1. *Bring and hold the boat directly before the wind.*
2. *Haul in the main sheet* until the end of the boom is over the transom. The helmsman must concentrate on rigid rudder control to keep the boat before the wind.
3. *Ease the tiller away from the sail* until the wind catches the back of the sail and swings it across to the opposite side. (Warn the crew to keep their heads down and be prepared to shift their weight to the opposite side before starting the turn.)
4. *Immediately check the turning of the boat* with the rudder and bring the boat back on course before

the wind. This is the crucial part of jibing in strong winds. If the turning of the boat is not stopped as the sails swing over, there is likely to be a knockdown or a capsize before the sheets can be released.

5. *Ease the sheets for the new course.* If the sheet has been "snubbed" around a cleat or winch it can be eased off smoothly and with little physical strain. Painful rope burns can occur if an unsnubbed sheet is allowed to slide through the hands.

A controlled jibe in light air simply consists of hauling in on the boom by means of the sheet or by hand and swinging it over to the opposite side. If the breeze is strong enough to lift the boom, ease the sail out under control. An unrestrained, free-swinging jibe, even in light air, can place great strain on both standing and running rigging.

Sailing Wing and Wing

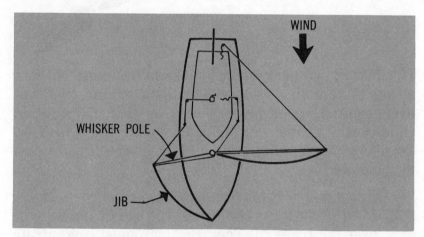

Headsails are likely to be "blanketed" by the main or other sails when running, unless the jib is brought over and the boat sailed *wing and wing.* A *whisker pole* is often used to "wing out" the jib to keep it from collapsing. The jib sheets are then adjusted to keep the sail at right angles to the wind. Tension on both sheets will also hold the pole in its fitting on the mast and hold its pin through the clew cringle. Remove the pole *before* changing to another course.

PICKING UP MOORINGS
AND LANDING AT PIERS

The approach to a pier or a mooring should be judged and timed so that at the moment of contact the boat is at or near a dead stop, but it should also be in a position to get under way and maneuver again in the event of a sudden wind shift, too much way on, or failure to pick up the mooring pendant. Boats respond differently to wind and wave conditions and they vary in the distance they will "carry," or coast, after they are headed into the wind or the sheets have been released. A boat with a heavy keel, for example, will have more momentum and will carry farther than a lightweight centerboarder traveling initially at the same speed. Approaches and simulated landings should be practiced under a variety of conditions until the handling characteristics of the boat are thoroughly understood. Practicing can best be done without danger of damaging the boat by mooring a small buoy or a life preserver in an open area and using it as a target for pickups (by a crewman from the bow using a boat-hook) and landings (coming alongside).

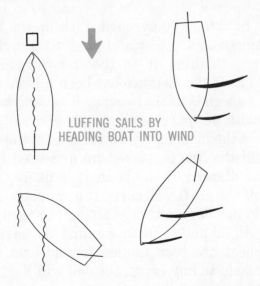

LUFFING SAILS BY
HEADING BOAT INTO WIND

A sailboat under way can be maneuvered to a stop by either heading and holding the boat directly into the wind to luff or spill the wind out of the sails or by releasing the sheets to luff the sails without changing the course of the boat if it is in any position from on a reach to sailing close-hauled. Generally, the practice is to head into the wind with the board down and drift in to reaching distance of the mooring or the pier. The following sequence is generally practiced in approaching and picking up a mooring or landing at a pier:

1. *Lower the centerboard.* The boat turns into the wind with better control with the board down. Also, the lowered board will help reduce speed during the approach.
2. *Lower and remove the jib.* Most sloops will sail and maneuver under the main alone. (How a boat handles without a jib should be determined before attempting to pick up a mooring in a crowded anchorage.) Bag the sail and secure the jib halyards.
3. *Approach the mooring or pier from the downwind side.* Head the boat directly into the wind when it is two or three boat lengths away from the mooring. Heavy keelboats will generally carry three or more boat lengths into the wind.
4. *Pick up and secure the mooring line.* Use a boathook to extend your reach. Pick up the line from a position near the bow and pass it through the chock before attaching it to the mooring bit or cleat. (NOTE. If the distance has been misjudged and the boat's speed is likely to carry it several boat lengths beyond a buoyed mooring, it is generally advisable to pass the mooring by and make another approach. Should the line be picked up and used to snub the forward speed of the boat, it is likely the momentum of the craft will carry it around the mooring in a wild 360-degree turn. During the turn, the mainsail will fill and come up against the shrouds unless the sheet has been hauled in and held during the approach. In any event, the sail will jibe, often with disasterous results, as the boat completes its swing around the buoy.)
5. *Lower and remove the mainsail.* Take out the bat-

tens and bag the sail. Place the boom in its crutch or adjust the topping lift to carry the boom's weight. Haul the main sheet in to hold the boom in place, then coil and suspend it from the boom.

6. *Remove and stow the rudder and tiller.*
7. *Bail out the boat.*
8. *Raise the centerboard* before leaving the craft. (NOTE. In a strong breeze, it may be advisable to raise the board as soon as the mooring line is picked up to prevent the boat from yawing or sailing around the mooring. On the other hand, some boats will ride better at their moorings if the board is partially lowered.)
9. *Double check all mooring lines* and protect them with chafing gear where they pass through chocks.
10. *Secure halyards* to prevent their slatting against the mast.
11. *Put sailbags and other gear into the dinghy.*
12. *Replace the cockpit cover if one is used.*

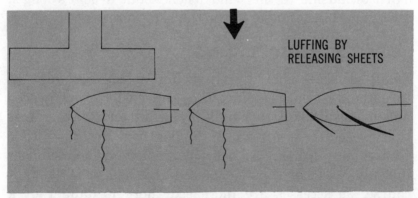

LUFFING BY
RELEASING SHEETS

It is not always possible, and in some instances not advisable, to head the boat into the wind when approaching a mooring or a pier. In a crowded anchorage area, where space to maneuver would be needed in case of overshooting the buoy or going in irons or when the wind is at an angle to the pier, the approach may be made from a reaching or other "on the wind" sailing position. Hold the boat on course and release the sheets to allow the sails to luff during the approach. *Make sure the sheets are completely slack.* There is no danger of going in

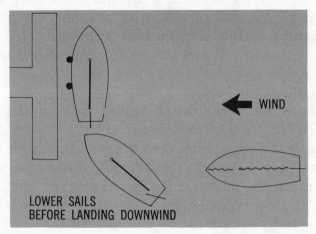

LOWER SAILS
BEFORE LANDING DOWNWIND

WIND

stays and if the boat should stop short of the mooring, it is a simple procedure to haul in on the sheets momentarily to get the extra drive needed to complete the approach. Pick up the mooring from the *windward* side of the boat. When it is necessary to land on the windward side of a pier, lower all the sails and drift in head on. Turn broadside to the wind when about a boat's length away and place fenders over the side to prevent chafing.

HEAVY WEATHER SAILING

Small sailboats should seek shelter at the first sign of threatening weather, since they are easily overpowered and made difficult to handle by wind and wave forces that exceed those for which the boat was designed. (See section on weather.) An overpowered or mishandled boat in rough weather can be capsized or sailed under and, of course, as stresses are increased there is danger of a rigging or structural failure. Should it be necessary to go out in strong wind, reduce sail area beforehand. Most sloops can be sailed under the main alone, but the jib is often carried for better balance if the mainsail can be shortened by reefing. On boats equipped with roller reefing gear, the lower part of the sail is simply cranked around the boom like a window shade as the halyard is slacked off, but with conventional rigs the sail is reefed by tying a section along the foot to the boom with a reefing line or reef points.

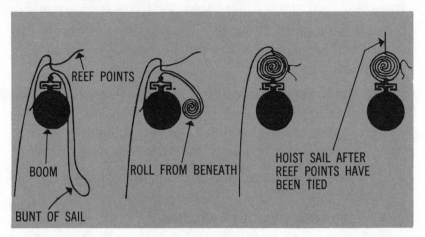

REEF POINTS

BOOM

BUNT OF SAIL

ROLL FROM BENEATH

HOIST SAIL AFTER
REEF POINTS HAVE
BEEN TIED

Reef the sail before hoisting it. Start at the mast end of the line of reef points and secure the tack *reef cringle* to the gooseneck fitting. Next, secure a line to the clew reef cringle at the leech end of the sail and pass it through the outhaul fitting and back through the cringle. Haul out the line of points, *hand taut,* and tie the cringle firmly to the boom.

Next, fold the section of the sail between the line of reef points and the foot and roll it tightly, *from beneath,* toward the boom. Pass the reef points or reefing line, working aft from the mast, around the rolled-up section of sail and secure them. Tie the points with a reef, or square knot, or a slipped reef knot.

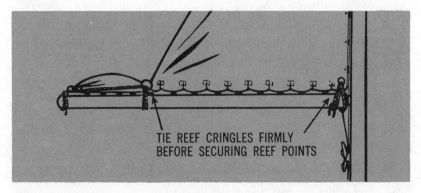

TIE REEF CRINGLES FIRMLY
BEFORE SECURING REEF POINTS

On rigs fitted with track and slides, the reef points are passed *between* the bolt rope and the boom. On slotted spars, the points are tied around the boom.

Raise the sail slowly and check each point carefully to be sure the tension along the line of points is evenly distributed. The reef is *shaken out* by reversing the reefing procedure.

If the wind velocity steadily increases before the boat can return to shelter and threatens to exceed the force the craft can safely handle, take the following precautions progressively as heavy weather conditions develop.

1. *When close reaching or beating to a point of safety—*
- Move crew weight to windward.
- Keep an eye to windward for signs (catspaws) of increased wind strength.
- Luff the boat, or ease the sheets in the stronger puffs to reduce wind pressure on the sails. Important: keep the boat moving, otherwise, rudder control will be lost.
- Put on life preservers.
- Keep the bilges dry. Water in the bilge will decrease stability.
- Lower the jib.
- Under extreme conditions, lower the mainsail and anchor if possible. Keep all weight low in the boat near or aft of amidship so that the bow can lift with the waves.
- Put out a drag, or *drogue*, if it is not possible to anchor. The sails can be bundled and tied to a line from the bow to reduce leeward drift.
- Stay with the boat in case of swamping or capsizing. (See section on safety and rescue.)

2. *When reaching to a point of safety, as when on the wind—*
- Keep weight to windward, bilges dry, life preservers on, and the boat moving.
- Ease the main sheet in the stronger puffs.
- Sheet the jib in tightly to back-wind the mainsail and reduce its drive. Also raise the centerboard

slightly if there is an excessive weather helm that may cause damage to the rudder assembly.

- Head the boat upwind of the objective to compensate for drift and to avoid taking the larger waves broadside.
- Drop and secure the mainsail. Most sloops can reach under the jib alone.
- Drop all sails and anchor or put out a drogue as under extreme conditions when on the wind.

3. *When broad reaching or running to a point of safety—*

   The boat is generally in a safer sailing position when reaching or running than when on the wind. Chief dangers are in broaching or turning broadside to wind and waves and in surfing down the face of a wave and burying the bow under the wave ahead. True wind velocity is deceptive while running, since the apparent wind is reduced by the speed of the boat. Consequently, high waves may develop before the true force of the wind is realized. Proceed as follows—

- Raise the centerboard to reduce the danger of broaching.
- Flatten the jib.
- On a broad reach, ease the main sheet until the boom is almost touching the shrouds.
- On a run, haul in the main to reduce wind pressure. The boat *must* be held directly before the wind to avoid sailing by the lee and the danger of an accidental jibe.
- Lower the main and sail by jib alone. This action can be taken while running if rudder control is good. Hold the boat directly before the wind and sheet the main in until the boom is near the center of the transom. Because of pressure on the sail, it may be necessary to haul the sail down by the bolt rope as the halyard is eased off.

- Flatten the jib and trail a line or drogue over the stern to reduce speed.
- Lower the jib and sail under bare poles.
- Anchor or ride to a drogue attached to the bow.

When it is necessary to ride out a blow, avoid a lee shore and try to work the boat to the leeward side of a headland or island where it may be possible to anchor in comparative shelter.

ANCHORING

Although boats are designed to move through the water with the least resistance possible, perhaps the most important equipment aboard is designed to prevent them from moving at all. Every boat should carry some type of anchoring device that can be relied upon to keep the boat in a restricted area without danger of dragging.

The selection of an anchor and anchor line is based upon the displacement of the boat, the amount of its resistance to wind and current drag, and the condition of the local mooring or the holding ground. Experienced boatmen who are familiar with the area can give authoritative advice. Nylon fiber, because of its strength, elasticity, and resistance to moisture and marine life, is first choice for anchor rodes. A ⅜-inch line of 100 feet or more, depending upon local conditions, is generally recommended for small sail craft. When in good condition, a nylon line of less than ⅜-inch diameter would probably have sufficient strength, but would be hard on the hands when it had to be pulled in under tension. A ½-inch rode would be easier on the hands.

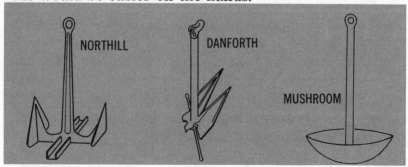

NORTHILL   DANFORTH   MUSHROOM

A lightweight anchor, such as the Danforth or the North-ill, has excellent holding qualities under most bottom conditions once it has been set. However, broad, fluked anchors have a tendency to "ski" over grassy bottoms and demand special care in setting.

The mushroom anchor is popular for sand and mud bottoms. In the larger sizes it is often used for permanent moorings.

A short length of chain between the anchor and the line, or rode, will increase the efficiency of any anchor and will also protect the line from chafe. A metal thimble in the eye-splice protects the rode from chafing at the shackle. The weight of the chain should equal or exceed that of the anchor.

When anchoring, remove the jib and approach the anchorage area with the bow into the wind. Check to be sure the anchor rode is secured to the boat and is free to run without fouling. When the boat comes to a stop, lower the anchor hand-over-hand until it touches bottom. Keep a slight tension on the rode as the boat drops back with the wind or the current until sufficient scope has been established. Give the rode several sharp tugs to set the anchor. Establish a range by lining up two landmarks on shore and check it frequently to determine whether the anchor is holding.

The general rule for anchoring is to have the scope of the anchor rode 5 to 10 times the depth of the water, depending upon wave and bottom conditions. Heavy-keel boats require more scope than centerboards, and the scope should be increased during heavy weather.

Attach a trip line to the crown of an anchor when bottom conditions are unknown or known to be foul and protect the anchor rode with chafing gear where it passes through the chock or over the edge of the gunwale. A split section of a rubber or a plastic hose can be slipped over the rode, or the rode may be wrapped with several layers of canvas. Use a light line or "small stuff" to keep the chafing gear in place.

To raise or hoist the anchor, shorten the scope until the boat is directly over the anchor. A steady pull will usually break it loose, but it may be necessary to take a turn or two around the mooring cleat with the shortened rode and break the anchor out under sail.

RULES OF THE ROAD

There are marine traffic laws for boats as there are highway traffic laws for automobiles, and, like the auto regulations, those for boat traffic vary according to locality. There are four sets of marine traffic laws—known as Rules of the Road—in effect in various geographical locations in and around the United States: (1) International, (2) Inland, (3) Great Lakes, and (4) Western Rivers. Detailed information concerning lights, signals, and passing maneuvers for each division is contained in three separate Coast Guard publications. The International and Inland rules are in Coast Guard Pamphlet CG-169. Those for the Great Lakes are in CG-172. The Western Rivers rules are found in CG-184. The pamphlets are available from local Coast Guard Marine Inspection Offices or may be ordered from Coast Guard Headquarters, Washington, D.C.

Under the rules, sailing craft have the right of way over powered craft unless they are overtaking a powered vessel. However, it is prudent for small sailboats to keep out of the way of large heavy vessels that are difficult to stop or maneuver. The revised International Rules (September 1965) also deny the right of sailing craft in a narrow channel to hamper the safe passage of a power driven vessel that can navigate only inside such a channel. When two sailboats are near each other and there is danger of colliding, one (the burdened vessel) must keep clear of the other (the privileged vessel). Four main situations are recognized (except under the 1965 International Rules):

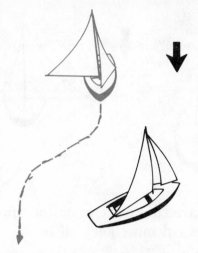

1. A sailboat running free must keep clear of one close hauled.

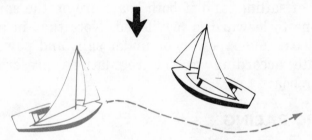

2. A sailboat close hauled on the port tack must keep clear of one close hauled on the starboard tack.

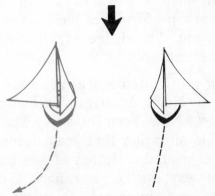

3. When both boats are running free on opposite tacks, the vessel with the wind on the port side must keep clear.

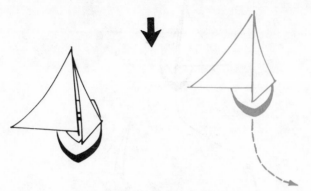

4. If both boats are running free on the same tack, the boat to windward must keep clear.

Under the revised International Rules, a boat on the starboard tack has the right of way, regardless of the point of sailing, and if both boats are on the same tack, the one to leeward is privileged. Note that in all rules, a sailboat under power, or under sails and power, must operate according to the regulations prescribed for motor boats.

BASIC RACING

Sailing in competition with other boats of the same class is an excellent way to "sharpen up" sailing skills after the fundamentals have been learned. Competition not only helps to develop a sensitivity to those conditions that effect a boat's performance but also is an exercise in which judgment, knowledge of right-of-way rules, tactics, and sportsmanship play an important part.

Sailing races in the United States are conducted under the rules set by the North American Yacht Racing Union, 37 West 44th St., New York 36, N.Y. The rules cover every conceivable situation that may develop during a race, but only a brief description of the basic ones involving right of way can be given here. Certain definitions are necessary to interpret the rules:

1. *Start.* When, after starting signal, any part of the hull, crew, or equipment crosses the starting line in

the direction of the first mark.

2. *Finish.* When any part of the hull, or equipment *in normal position*, crosses the finishing line in the direction of the last mark.

3. *Mark.* An object a boat must round or pass on a specified side. It marks the beginning, end, or boundary of a course or "leg."

5. *Clear astern.* When no part of a boat or her equipment in normal position is forward of a line projected abeam from the aftermost part of another boat. The other boat is clear ahead.

8. *Luffing.* Altering course toward the wind until head to wind.

10. *Proper course.* Any course sailed after the start, in the absence of other boats affected, to finish as quickly as possible. (Luffing or bearing off to prevent another boat from passing is not a proper course.)

Right-of-Way Rules

A foul is committed when a rule has been violated. The boat is automatically disqualified and the skipper must drop out of the race immediately if he is aware of the violation. Right-of-way rules are as follows:

1. *When on opposite tacks.* The port tack boat shall keep clear.

2. *When on the same tack.* The boat to windward must keep clear of the boat to leeward. (This applies when on a beat, reach or run but only when the boats overlap and are within two boat lengths of each other.)

3. *When passing mark.* If boats overlap, the outside boat must give the inside boat "buoy room" to round or pass the mark.

4. *When tacking or jibing.* A boat must keep clear of other boats when coming about or jibing.

Before the Start

1. *When altering course on the same tack.* A boat

clear ahead or to leeward may alter course. The change in course must be done *slowly* if it would affect another boat.

2. *When on the same tack* (anti-barging rule). A leeward boat does not have to give a windward boat room to *pass* between her and the starting mark.
3. *When over the line at the start.* A boat over the line before the start must keep clear of all other boats and return for a restart.

After Starting

1. *When on the same tack luffing.* A boat may luff another that is clear astern or to windward, until the helmsman of the windward boat comes abreast of the mainmast of the leeward boat.
2. *When on the same tack, bearing away.* A boat may not sail below her normal course when reaching or running to prevent a leeward boat from passing.

All boats must do their utmost to prevent collisions regardless of any right-of-way situation.

Racing Courses

A triangular course that provides for a beat, a reach, and a run is the most popular layout for sailing races, although a windward-leeward arrangement is often used. The starting line is usually between an anchored race committee boat and a fixed mark, and at or near a right angle to the first mark. The first leg should be a beat to windward, otherwise, boats making a good start are likely to be "blanketed" by those starting late. After the start, the committee boat usually moves to establish a finish line at right angles to the last leg of the course. (Racing tactics and strategy are too involved to be covered here. Many excellent references are available, and local sailing groups or individuals can be contacted for information and guidance.)

WEATHER

The experienced sailor develops a healthy respect for weather conditions and is constantly alert to changes in temperature, wind direction, cloud formation, and barometric pressure, any of which may indicate the approach of bad weather. Weather predictions based on local observation, however, are usually in the short-range category and are of greatest value in forecasting localized weather phenomena, such as thunderstorms. For long-range predictions, the official Weather Bureau forecasts give the most reliable information on what can be expected in weather changes. Long-range predictions are published in the daily papers and are broadcast throughout the day and night by radio stations and should be checked carefully before starting an outing on the water.

The weather forecast includes changes that may be expected to take place in temperature, humidity, precipitation, visibility, and wind velocity. Of greatest concern to sailors from a safety standpoint are wind velocity and, to a lesser degree, visibility. Large weather systems that produce high wind velocities are carefully plotted and accurately forecast in time to prepare for or avoid their approach.

Localized thunderstorms are generally the most dangerous weather menace to small craft. Towering cloud formations with dark bases should be looked for when they are predicted for the area. They may form quickly and can develop squalls with wind velocities of 50 miles per hour or more. Fortunately, they are slow-moving and small in size—about 1 to 10 miles in diameter—and do not last long. The alert and cautious observer seeks shelter long before the vicious "sudden" storms strike.

Thunderstorms also develop along the advancing front of a cold air mass when it meets warm, humid air. They may extend in a line of several hundred miles, and until they have passed, small craft should remain in port. Transistor radios can be carried aboard the smallest boats. They offer the best means of keeping posted afloat on weather conditions. They may also warn of thunderstorms in the vicinity by emitting static noises.

Lightning is an added danger to sailboats during thunderstorms. If the storm cannot be avoided, every effort should be made to get as close to shore as possible, where objects at a higher elevation than the mast are most likely to be hit by the electrical discharge. If caught out in open water in advance of or during a thunderstorm, keep as low in the boat as possible and away from the mast and standing rigging.

The wind-barometer table compiled for the territory of the United States by the Weather Bureau, reproduced below, may be of help to the sailor in predicting the weather when official forecasts are not available.

Wind-barometer Table

Wind Direction	Barometer Reduced to Sea Level	Character of Weather
SW to NW	30.10 to 30.20 and steady	Fair, with slight temperature changes for 1 or 2 days.
SW to NW	30.10 to 30.20 and rising rapidly	Fair followed by rain within 2 days.
SW to NW	30.20 and above and stationary	Continued fair with no decided temperature change.
SW to NW	30.20 and above, falling slowly	Slowly rising temperature, fair for 2 days.
S to SE	30.10 to 30.20, falling slowly	Rain within 24 hours.
S to SE	30.10 to 30.20, falling rapidly	Wind increasing in force, with rain within 12 to 24 hours.
SE to NE	30.10 to 30.20, falling slowly	Rain in 12 to 18 hours.
SE to NE	30.10 to 30.20, falling rapidly	Increasing wind and rain within 12 hours.
E to NE	30.10 and above, falling slowly	In summer, with light winds, rain may not fall for several days. In winter, rain in 24 hours.
E to NE	30.10 and above, falling fast	In summer, rain probably in 12 hours. In winter, rain or snow, with increasing winds, will often set in when the barometer begins to fall and the wind sets in NE.
SE to NE	30.00 or below, falling slowly	Rain will continue 1 or 2 days.
SE to NE	30.00 or below, falling rapidly	Rain with high wind, followed within 36 hours by clearing, and in winter, colder.
S to SW	30.00 or below, rising slowly	Clearing in a few hours, fair several days.
S to E	29.80 or below, falling rapidly	Severe storm imminent, followed in 24 hours by clearing, and in winter, colder.
E to N	29.80 or below, falling rapidly	Severe NE gale and heavy rain; in winter, heavy snow and a cold wave.
Going to W	29.80 or below, rising rapidly	Clearing and colder.

NOTE. The table includes general statements about the weather and can be very useful. However, the latest official Weather Bureau forecast should be used whenever the forecast is available. These forecasts are available on scheduled marine radioplane broadcasts, from commercial radio stations, and from the Weather Bureau offices.

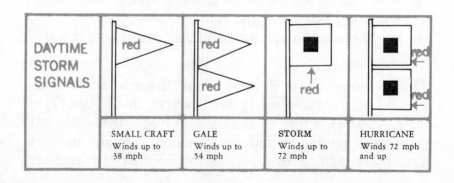

78

The development of rope, especially in the larger sizes, was an essential element in the evolution of ships and the expansion of exploration and commerce. Prehistoric man used vines or strips of grass, bark, or animal skin for holding and tying purposes, and early cultures soon discovered that larger and stronger bonds could be made by plaiting and twisting quantities of animal or vegetable fibers together. The rope-making materials varied with the regions. The Egyptians used papyrus and flax (linen) fibers, and nomadic tribes made ropes of horsehair and rawhide. The Chinese used silk as well as bamboo fibers, and in the remote areas of Oceania, braided sennit is still made from the fibers of the coconut.

There has been little change in the specialized art of ropemaking since the beginning of recorded history, with the exception that machines have replaced manual labor, and man-made fibers now compete with many of those used by the first sailors.

Of the vegetable fibers, manila (from the abaco plant of the Philippines) and sisal are still widely used in ropemaking, and lines of linen (flax), cotton, hemp, and jute have specalized uses aboard sailboats; but the synthetic fibers of nylon, dacron, polyethylene, and polypropylene, because of their strength and resistance to moisture, mildew, and water organisms, have largely replaced natural fibers in marine rope.

There are two basic types of rope, laid and braided. The laid is the most common and consists of natural or synthetic fibers laid parallel to form *slivers*, which in turn are twisted into yarns. The yarns are then twisted in the opposite direction from the slivers to form strands, and the strands (generally three) are given a reverse twist to form the rope. By reversing the twist each time, the three parts are balanced, and the tendency to untwist and come apart is overcome.

In some ropes made for special purposes, the strands

spiral upward and to the left when the rope is held in a vertical position, but for the most part they are made to twist to the right. The manner of coiling, and, to a degree, the use of a line is affected by the right- or left-hand twists given to the strands. Laid rope is made in diameters of 3/16 to 4 inches. Cables are formed when larger sizes are needed by twisting three ropes together in the opposite direction from the strands of the rope.

Braided rope is made in either a hollow or a solid form. The hollow form is generaly made of eight braided strands of synthetic fibers. In the solid forms, the braids are made around a core of parallel strands or around a braid core of the hollow type. Eight or sixteen strands are generally used in the solid types of braided rope.

Rope

SELECTION OF ROPE

Rope used for specific purposes aboard a boat is called a *line* and is usually selected on the basis of tensile strength, elasticity, and resistance to abrasion, rot, and marine life and to a degree on the basis of cost. Strength is generally the primary consideration when selecting rope, but size and flexibility are also important. For example, synthetic ropes of small diameters are often strong enough for sheets on small boats but when used are likely to slip through or cut the hands when hauled in under tension. Correct size and flexibility are also necessary when the lines run through blocks or fairleads.

Elasticity—or the lack of it—must be taken into account when choosing a rope for a specific purpose. The stretch qualities of nylon make it ideal for anchor rodes and mooring lines where its "shock-absorption" action reduces strain on fittings, gear, and hull. Dacron and manila, on the other hand, are often used for sheets and halyards because of their little-or-no-stretch characteristics.

It is generally recommended that the rated breaking strength of rope should exceed by about five times the weight or pull it might be subjected to. The anchor rode for an 800-pound sailboat, for example, should have a strength specification of approximately 4,000 pounds. The 5-to-1 safety factor would take care of possible overloads and would also compensate somewhat for normal wear and deterioration of the line.

TYPES OF ROPE

The following chart on rope specifications and information on the characteristics of the various kinds of rope may be of help in making a satisfactory selection. Note that two or more types are often suitable for the same purpose and also keep in mind that the quality of any rope will vary with the grade of fiber used in the construction.

TENSILE STRENGTH IN POUNDS
APPROXIMATE AVERAGE

Size	Manila	Nylon	Dacron	Poly-ethylene	Poly-propylene
3/16″	450	1,100	1,350	700	800
1/4″	600	1,950	2,250	1,200	1,350
5/16″	1,000	2,960	3,450	1,750	1,960
3/8″	1,350	4,200	4,700	2,500	2,650
1/2″	2,650	7,200	8,000	4,100	4,200
3/4″	5,400	15,300	16,400	7,800	8,200
1″	9,000	26,500	26,300	13,300	14,000

Manila

Manila is an all-purpose rope made in several grades. The fibers have a natural protective lubrication but are usually treated with preservatives to resist rot and marine life. Manila rope has a lower initial cost than synthetics but is not as strong size for size and must be kept as dry as possible for long life. It has some elasticity and is often used for mooring and anchor lines. The better grades are used for sheets, halyards, and other running rigging.

Cotton

Cotton lines are soft, pliable, and easy to handle except when wet. They are used mostly in small sizes for flag halyards and lanyards. Their use has been largely replaced aboard boats by the use of synthetics.

Nylon

Nylon has superior strength (it is more than twice as strong as manila) as well as a stretch characteristic with a high recovery quality. It is rot- and mildew-proof, easy to handle, and highly resistant to abrasion. Nylon is excellent for anchor and mooring lines, although it loses about 10 percent of its strength when wet. It is considered to be too elastic for sheets and halyards, especially on larger boats.

Dacron

Dacron retains its full strength when wet and has only a slight stretch under loads. It is as strong as nylon and has similar characteristics. It is used for sheets, halyards, and other running rigging.

Polyethylene and Polypropylene

Polyethylene, made in a variety of colors, has nearly twice the strength of manila and very little stretch. Its outstanding quality is floatability. For this reason, it is popular for ski tow ropes and dinghy painters, where its use lessens the probability of fouling spinning propellers. It is adversely affected by heat and friction.

Polypropylene is much like polyethylene but has a higher melting point, is more abrasive-resistant, and is not as slippery. It is used mostly for water ski tow ropes and where low stretch is important.

The twisting action that takes place in rope-making subjects the fibers to great tension. Mishandling the line by kinking it or by bending it at sharp angles while it is under tension will add additional stress that may cause it to weaken or break down.

When not in use, mooring and other spare lines should be coiled and carefully stowed so as to be readily accessible. Lines of small diameter are coiled in the hand, larger ones on the deck. Loops of uniform size are cast clockwise to form the coil.

Each loop, as it is cast, is given a twist with the coiling hand to start it into a clockwise spiral.

Wet mooring and anchor lines should be *faked down* and allowed to dry before stowing. Although synthetic fibers are not affected by moisture, they could, if stowed wet, raise the humidity in the lockers and encourage mildew and dry rot. Protect the ropes, especially those made of vegetable fibers, from caustic agents and never store them near storage batteries.

Sand and dirt between the fibers of rope will have an abrasive effect if not rinsed off. The accumulation can best be removed by sloshing the line over the side or by towing it behind the boat for a few hundred yards. Water from a high pressure hose is not recommended, since it would force the dirt particles deeper into the rope. Towing a line behind the boat for a short distance will also help restore its "balance" if it has been kinked by mishandling. Whip or otherwise prevent the ends from becoming unlaid before trailing the line in the water.

Carefully check all lines periodically for cuts and abrasions and for mildew or rot if they are made of natural fibers. The surface condition of natural fiber can be deceptive.

Twist the rope to expose the inner surfaces of the strands. If they have a moldy or a dry, colorless appearance, it is a sign of deterioration, and the rope should be discarded. The life of sheets and other running rigging can be prolonged by occasionally switching the line end for end. In sailing it is important to remember that the safety of the boat and crew often depends upon the proper care and use of reliable lines.

WHIPPING, KNOT TYING, AND SPLICING

Whipping

The working lines aboard a boat will quickly take on a brushlike or cowtail appearance if the ends are not treated in some manner. "Irish pennants" are not only unsightly but also can dangerously become entangled with other lines and jam blocks in running rigging. The practice of taping or whipping the ends of the line is generally used to keep the strands from becoming unlaid, but the end of a synthetic line can also be treated by fusing the fibers together with a match flame.

Take a turn or two around the line with twine before heating the ends and carefully avoid contact with the molten tip or the droplets that may form and fall during the process. The end can be smoothed and shaped before it cools by drawing it across a rough surface such as concrete to remove the excess molten synthetic material.

Waterproof tape is sometimes used to hold the strands together, or the tip of a line can be dipped into an activated, quick-drying resin such as a polyester or an epoxy used in fiberglassing.

Some form of whipping is preferred by many sailors. Whipping twine of cotton or linen is usually doubled and rubbed with or pulled through a lump of beeswax to strengthen and weatherproof it before it is applied. (The weatherproofing quality of the wax can be improved by melting and mixing together 1 part powdered resin with 5 parts beeswax. Keep the heat low when melting the mixture, because the mixture is flammable. Pour the mixture in molds of muffin tin size to congeal and cool.) Larger line of ¾ inch or more is usually whipped with marlin (tarred Italian hemp).

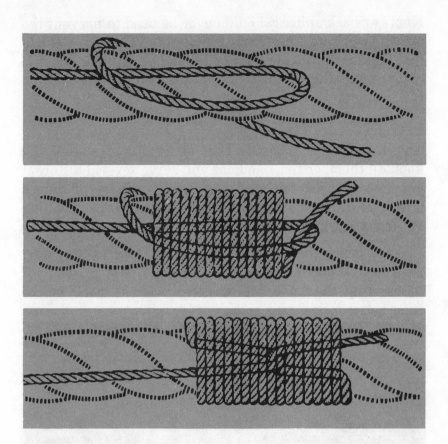

A temporary whipping can be put on quickly and will serve for a time until a more permanent type can be applied.

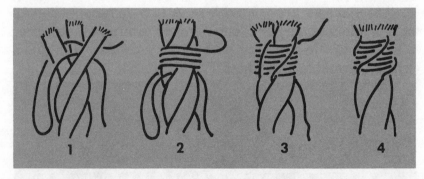

The sailmaker's whipping will withstand hard usage and is generally preferred for running rigging and mooring lines. It can be put on with or without a sail needle; however, the whipping will be more secure if it is sewn on.

Knots or back splices should never be used to prevent the ends of working lines from untwisting. The extra thickness would complicate knot tying and cleating and would make impossible the use of the line through blocks and fair-leaders.

Knot Tying

The use of lines aboard a boat generally involves tying knots in them. Often, one knot will serve several different purposes; consequently, a working knowledge of only a few essential knots is needed for efficient rope handling aboard a sailboat.

In knot tying the *running end* of the rope is that part used in making the knot. The *standing part* is not used in forming the knot, and the *bight* is the bend in the rope between the two ends.

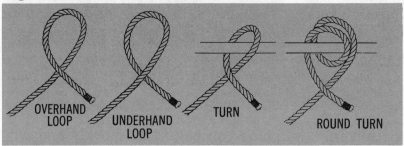

OVERHAND LOOP   UNDERHAND LOOP   TURN   ROUND TURN

To form an *overhand loop*, cross the running end over the standing part. The running end goes behind the standing part to make an *underhand loop*. A *turn* is taken when an overhand or underhand loop is made around an object or a section of the standing part and a *round turn* is taken when a second loop is added.

STANDING PART   RUNNING END   OVERHAND KNOT

The overhand knot is the simplest of all knots. It is sometimes used as a "stopper knot" in the end of a line, but it jams easily and is hard to untie.

FIGURE EIGHT KNOT

The figure eight knot makes the best stopper to keep the end of a line or sheet from running through a block or fair-leader. Tie it by bringing the end from an underhand loop over the standing part and back through the loop from beneath. Draw the end up snugly. The knot can also be used to attach rope halyards to the sails.

REEF KNOT

The square, or reef, knot is used in furling and reefing sails. To tie it, cross the ends over and under each other to form an overhand type of knot. Add a second overhand on top of the first. *In tying the second overhand, be sure the ends cross on the same side from which they emerged from the first overhand.* The unreliable and easy to jam granny knot will result if the ends are crossed incorrectly. A pull on one end will collapse the knot so that it can be untied easily.

SLIPPED REEF KNOT

The slipped reef knot is often used instead of the reef knot. It is easier to untie if it is wet or has been pulled up tightly. Never use a reef knot to join two rope ends together. Use a single or double sheet bend instead.

SHEET BEND

The sheet bend can also be used to join the end of a mooring line to the eye splice in the end of another line (Becket hitch). In joining lines of unequal diameter, pass the smaller line through and around the eye or bight of the larger. Use a double sheet bend on synthetic lines.

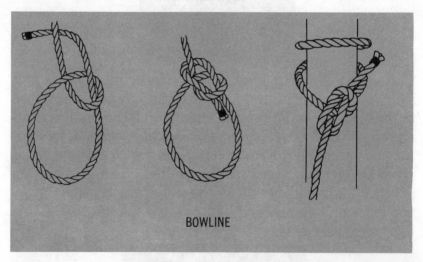

BOWLINE

A temporary loop in the end of a line can be formed with a bowline.

If a bowline is used to tie up to a piling or to secure an anchor line around the base of the mast, take a round turn before tying the bowline. Although the bowline will not slip or jam, it cannot be tied in a line already under tension or untied while there is stress applied. A round turn and two half hitches would be better for use under tension.

ROUND TURN AND
TWO HALF HITCHES

The round turn is made clockwise around a piling (twice around), and two half hitches are taken around the standing part of a line. Pass the running end under the standing part in forming the half hitches. This procedure allows the end of the line to hang naturally and, to a degree, prevents the hitches from loosening up. Note that the half hitches form a clove hitch around the standing part of the line.

THE ANCHOR, OR
FISHERMAN'S, BEND

The anchor, or fisherman's, bend is similar to the round turn and two half hitches and is often used to secure a line to an anchor. The first half hitch around the standing part also "picks up" the round turn. This is an excellent knot for use under tension, but the end should be *seized* to the standing part if the tension is not continuous.

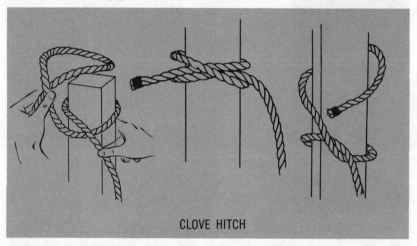

CLOVE HITCH

Two underhand loops can be slipped over a pole to form a clove hitch. The clove hitch is often used for mooring a small boat but it should not be trusted or left unattended for long periods of time.

The clove hitch can also be formed by taking two round turns about a piling. Pass the running end beneath the first turn and take the second turn above the first with the end again passing underneath. Unless there is steady tension on the line, the clove hitch may loosen or come adrift completely. Loosening can be prevented by adding two half hitches around the standing part of the line.

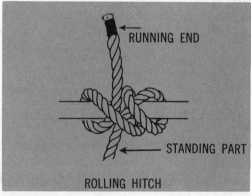

RUNNING END

STANDING PART

ROLLING HITCH

The rolling hitch is a more dependable knot than a clove hitch and is more often used when attaching a line to a smooth surface or to a larger rope. The pull can be paral-

lel or at an angle. To tie the knot, take two turns around
the spar, overlapping the standing part each time. Con-
tinue with a third turn around and bring the running
end up under the second turn and adjacent to the standing part.

SPLICING

Short Splice

A sheet bend is a temporary means of joining two ropes.
Splices are used for permanent joinings. The short splice
is very strong but it doubles the diameter of the rope and
cannot be used if the line has to pass through a correctly
sized block or fair-leader.

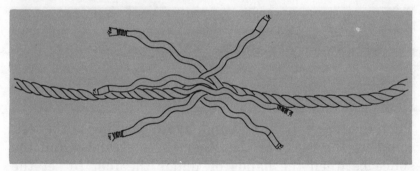

In step 1, unlay the ends about 6 inches and individually
whip and alternately space the strands as the ends are
brought together. In step 2, use a tight seizing to hold
the two ends where they join.

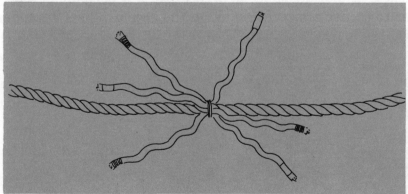

Start on the left and tuck each strand in turn over and
under the three strands in the standing part of the line.

Rotate the splice away from you as each strand goes down where the preceding one comes up. Three tucks are sufficient for natural fiber ropes, but at least five should be taken in synthetic lines.

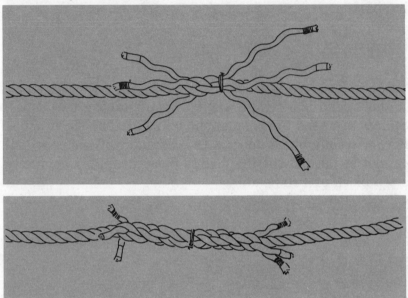

Turn the rope end for end and, again working to the left, complete the tucks of the other three strands. Roll the splice between the hands or under the foot to set the strands before trimming. *Do not cut off the ends too close.*

Eye Splice

The eye, or side, splice is used to form a permanent loop or to secure a metal thimble in the end of a line. Tempo-

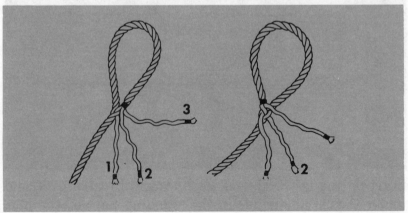

rary whippings are generally applied as indicated after the strands are unlaid (four turns for a three tuck or six turns for a five tuck).

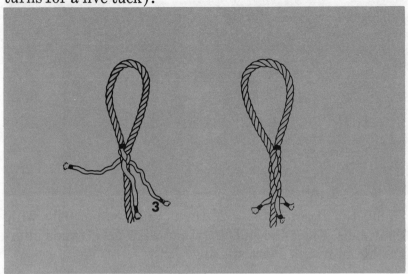

When the unlaid end is bent around to form the eye, have the center strand on top of the "Y" formed by the other two. Untwist the rope where the splice will begin and insert number 1 against the lay and under any one of the three separated strands in the standing part. Tuck number 2, the center strand, under the next strand down from number 1. Note that number 2 goes down where number 1 comes up. Strand number 3 goes down where number 2 comes up and tucks under the third strand in the standing part of the line. Pull each strand gently, in turn, to seat it snugly before repeating the series of tucks in the same order beginning with strand number 1. After the final series of tucks, roll the splice under the foot or between the hands to seat the strands evenly.

The splice can be tapered by cutting a few yarns out of each strand after each series of tucks. After each tuck, twist the strands to preserve the original lay of the rope.

Long Splice

The long splice is weaker than the short splice, but the diameter of the line remains the same.

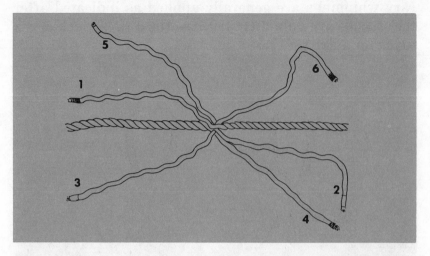

Unlay the strands 15 to 20 turns and temporarily whip their ends. Place the ends together with the strands alternating as in the short splice.

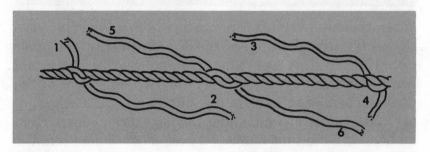

Unlay one strand and replace it with its counterpart from the other end as 1 and 2 in step 1 above. Repeat in the opposite direction with 3 and 4.

Tie each pair with an overhand knot and tuck each strand in twice as in the short splice.

Cleating

To secure the free end of a line to a cleat, take a turn clockwise around the base of the cleat and then a figure-of-eight turn over and under each horn. The last turn is made by casting a half hitch over the horn. In forming the half hitch, be sure the running end of the line is in front of the bight, or loop, before the bight is flipped over the horn of the cleat. When cleated properly, the line

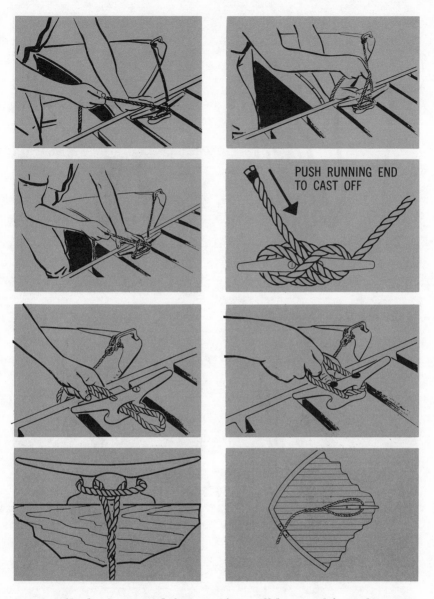

PUSH RUNNING END
TO CAST OFF

can easily be loosened for casting off by pushing the running end toward the half hitch. The bight of a bowline or an eye splice should be just large enough to slip under one horn of the cleat and then under the other. A larger loop might accidentally slip off unless a round turn is taken about the cleat. The mooring line can be securely fastened to hollow-base cleats by inserting the bight through the hole and then doubling it back over the horns.

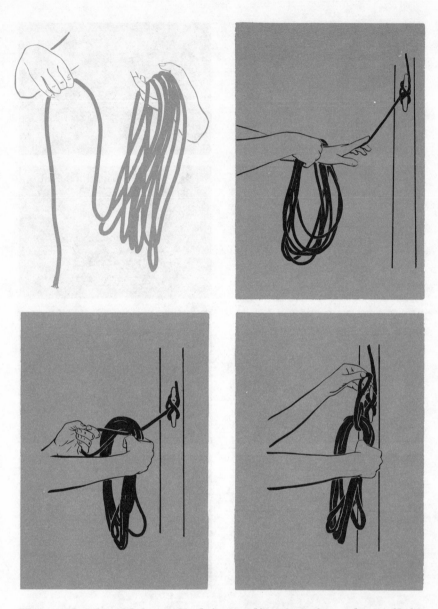

Halyards should be coiled immediately after the sail is hoisted and hung on the cleat. Start the coil next to the cleat and reach through and pick up the center of the standing part after the coil has been completed. Twist the bight formed in the standing part a turn or two and slip it over the cleat. When lowering the sail, place the coil face down on the deck so that the halyard is free to run without fouling.

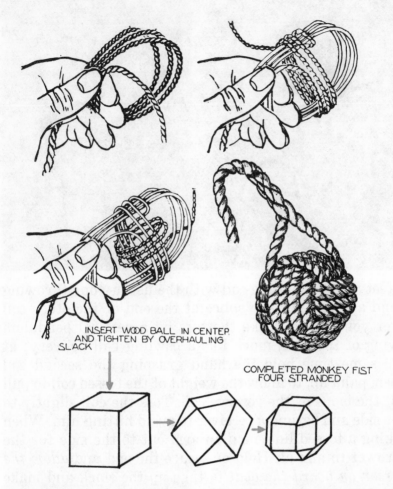

INSERT WOOD BALL IN CENTER.
AND TIGHTEN BY OVERHAULING
SLACK

COMPLETED MONKEY FIST
FOUR STRANDED

A 60-foot ¼-inch manila heaving line with a *monkey fist* worked into one end is easy to coil and toss. The slight additional weight will carry it well in a cross wind, but the monkey fist is not so heavy that it will injure a person accidentally struck by it. The line should be kept handy for rescue purposes, and it can be used as a "messenger" to get another line that is too heavy to toss across a wide open space.

An eye splice large enough to slip over the hands at the opposite end of the line will prevent accidentally losing the line during the toss. To heave the line, split the coil and drop one loop so that the half coils can be held about

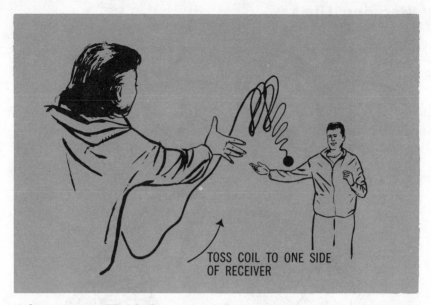

TOSS COIL TO ONE SIDE
OF RECEIVER

5 feet apart. Hold the coil with the fist in your throwing hand and slip the eye splice at the end of the other coil over your wrist. Make the toss by a vertical pendulum swing of the arm, much like a bowling ball delivery; at the same time hold the hand grasping the second coil open, palm up, to allow the weight of the tossed coil to pull out the loops of the reserve coil. Toss the coil slightly to one side and beyond a receiver to avoid hitting him. When taking a tossed line, hold an arm out to the side for the thrower to aim at. Hold or secure the end and *allow the person on board the boat* to take up the slack and make all adjustments.

For simplicity, the first three drawings show the steps in making a three-stranded fist. A fourth loop is added to make the more popular four-stranded fist shown in the fourth drawing.

To tighten the knot around the core, feed back the slack, one loop after the other, without allowing the loops to become misplaced. The tightening process usually requires three stages. A pair of pointed pliers is helpful in picking up the slack in the final "go-round." Eye splice the running end back into the line to complete the operation.

Capsizing and falling overboard have been the cause of approximately 65 percent of all fatal accidents in outboards and about 46 percent in cabin-type motorboats. The overboard accident, however, is not an uncommon experience in sailing and, for the most part, the participants expect and are prepared for an occasional dunking. Generally speaking, embarrassment and perhaps temporary discomfort are the major concern of these "victims."

Most sailing mishaps are caused by failure to note changes in wind conditions or by waiting too long to shorten sail and take other precautions in the face of an approaching squall. Sheets that are tightly cleated or fouled or that cannot be released immediately also account for many capsizes.

The fact that fewer lives are lost in sailboats as compared with other types of small craft—about 3 percent of the total, although sailboats make up 7 percent of the recreational small craft fleet—is largely due to the practice of teaching sailing in organized classes where swimming ability is a requisite and overboard work is part of the training in seamanship.

Sailboats with fixed heavy keels are likely to sink (founder) if filled with water unless sufficient reserve bouyancy in the hull has been provided for. Wooden centerboard boats, on the other hand, or boats with bouyancy compartments, will remain at the surface if filled with water.

Although the definition of capsize is "upset," or "overturn," the typical centerboard decked-over sailboat usually remains on its side when "capsized." Members of the crew are often able to climb to and remain on the high side, but their weight, unless it is balanced properly, may force the boat over into a true capsize position and complicate the rescue. The following step-by-step procedure for a capsize drill can be modified, when necessary, to meet most capsize situations:

1. Stay with the boat and check immediately for the safety of the crew. Put on life jackets and have the crew hang on to the centerboard to keep the boat on its side. Do not attempt to swim for shore unless the boat is drifting into a danger area or the water is extremely cold. A boat is easier to spot by rescuers than a swimmer would be.
2. Place a buoyant cushion or an extra life jacket under the tip of a metal mast if there is a tendency for the boat to roll upside down.
3. Avoid swimming movements, especially of the legs when moving about. There is less chance of getting tangled in sheets and other loose gear if the standing rigging, mast, or hull is used to pull yourself about.
4. Recover nearby floating items and push them under the bow or the stern deck. *Don't attempt to swim after gear that is floating away from the boat.*
5. Release the clew outhaul, sheets, and halyards. Secure *ends* of halyards to cleats.
6. Haul the mainsail down the mast but leave the halyard attached to the headboard.
7. Haul down the jib but do not remove it from the stay.
8. Remove the buoyant device from the mast tip.
9. Have the crew pull or climb on the centerboard to to right the boat.
10. Keep the boat upright by hanging onto the gunwales.
11. Secure a tow line from the rescue boat to the base of the mast.
12. Enter the boat and sit on the bottom.
13. Haul in sheets, sails, and other gear.
14. Pull up and secure the centerboard.
15. Instruct the towing vessel to *proceed as slowly as possible.* (The rudder may be used to keep the swamped boat from yawing.)

It is usually advisable to have one or two of the crew remain with the swamped boat during the tow. Their weight should be kept as low as possible and toward the stern. To keep the craft from rolling over, it may be necessary to leave the boat and hang onto each quarter of the transom. If the top of the centerboard well is closed or above the water level and the boat has a drain plug at the bottom of the transom, the plug can be removed to allow the water to drain from the boat during the tow. The towing vessel can gradually increase speed as the water level drops, and it is sometimes possible to completely empty the boat in this fashion. Naturally, the plug must be replaced as soon as forward progress has stopped.

Damage is likely to occur to a swamped craft if its forward motion is stopped suddenly. The momentum of the water as it surges forward can open seams, split the hull, or rip off the deck. Gently beach the boat in shallow water, preferably on a soft or sandy bottom, and pump or bail the water out. It is not advisable to empty the boat by tipping it on its side. The weight of the water will place undue strain on the low side and gunwale and may, in the case of flat and V-bottom boats, open up the seam along the chine.

"Man Overboard!"

The sailboat skipper, in planning and carrying out a rescue of a victim who has fallen overboard, must take into account the circumstances and conditions that prevail at the time of the accident. Trained sailors have practiced simulated rescues under a variety of conditions and are able to initiate a course of action that will minimize the risks that are involved in a rescue operation. They know how important it is to have all equipment in top condition and ready for instant use. Also safety conscious skippers make a point of knowing the swimming capabilities of those on board and whether there are health and physical problems that would have to be considered in the event of an emergency. Essentially, there are only two basic rescue procedures. In one, a flotation device is tossed toward the victim and the boat is maneuvered back to make contact; and in the other, after the flotation device has been thrown toward the victim, the boat is stopped and the victim saves himself by swimming to the boat. The advantages of the second method are often overlooked, but, of course, its success is wholly dependent upon the victim's ability to take care of himself in the water and upon a previously agreed upon understanding that the boat would be "made dead in the water" to give the man overboard an opportunity to save himself.

The advantages and disadvantages of the self-rescue method follow:

1. *The boat, made immediately dead in the water, is kept near the accident scene.* Sails can be dropped and an anchor or drogue used to prevent drifting, if necessary.
2. *The boat can be seen by the victim.* This is extremely important if the accident occurs at night or in a confused or breaking sea. It is almost impossible to sight, even in daylight at close range, a small floating object as it appears at brief intervals at the crest of one wave in a sea of waves.
3. *Voice communication is usually possible* if auxiliary motors are not used for maneuvering.
4. *The victim is encouraged by his progress toward safety and in the knowledge that the boat will not leave the area.* During a search procedure that involves maneuvering the boat when the victim cannot be seen, there will be times when the boat will be moving *away* from the accident area. The victim's observation that the boat is moving away is likely to lead to frantic swimming efforts, panic, and early exhaustion.
5. *The danger of being run down by the rescue craft is eliminated.*

The self-rescue method is not possible when:

1. *The victim is unable to swim owing to an injury.* An accidental jibe may stun and knock a crewman

overboard. This accident would be one of the few reasons that would justify a second person's going overboard—with lifesaving gear—to support the victim. A nonswimmer in the water without buoyant support would also need immediate assistance.

2. *The operator is unable to keep the boat from making leeway in a high wind.*

When there is doubt about the ability of the person in the water to care for himself, the boat must be sailed back to the victim. Small sailboats can be quickly maneuvered under average sailing conditions and can return to the person in the water with little loss of time if correct procedures are followed. A lifesaving device should be immediately tossed to the victim, and a crew member should be instructed to keep his eye on the victim. During the change in course back to the victim, it is important to keep maximum way on for control and a fast recovery. The following diagramed maneuvers for small boats sailing under average conditions offer effective means for making rapid contact.

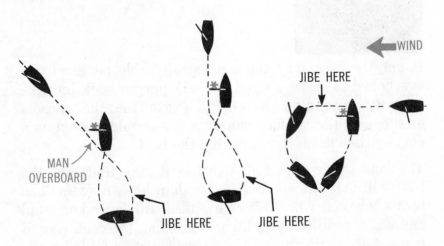

Reentering the Boat

Bring a victim aboard, if possible, forward of amidships, otherwise the bow is likely to fall off the wind, and the boat will get under way as the sails fill. It may be necessary to lower the sails before the victim can be brought aboard. A swimming ladder or a line with a loop in the end lowered over the side can be used as an aid in helping the person back aboard.

A person may be lifted from the water if the freeboard is low enough and he is not too heavy. Grasp his armpits from the rear and hoist him up to a sitting position on the gunwale or transom.

A heavier person can be assisted aboard by two people. He is lifted by the arms until he can be jackknifed over the gunwale.

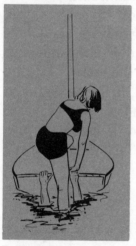

It may be necessary for a physically able person to go overboard to assist a tired or weak person back into the boat. By suspending himself full length from the transom or the side, the rescuer can have his shoulder used as a step by the victim in reentering the boat.

The lone sailor who falls overboard may find that the boat will drift downwind faster than he can swim. The boat's behavior when left unattended will depend on wind and water conditions and whether or not the centerboard is up. Also, if the main sheet was cleated or fouled while the boat was sailing close-hauled, the boat may head up into the wind and stop. It will then begin to drift back on its rudder and turn until the wind again fills the sail and drives it to windward. It may repeat the process over and over and give the victim a chance to intercept it as it alternately sails forward and falls back. (Large sailing craft purposely adjust sails and rudder in this manner when hove to in a storm. A boat will take care of itself when properly balanced.)

ARTIFICIAL RESPIRATION

Boats frequently operate in areas far from immediate medical attention, and it should be the concern of every boatman to be able to care for himself and others in the event of an accident or sudden illness. Training in emergency first aid procedures is offered free of charge by most Red Cross chapters.

Because of the environment, users of small craft may encounter life-threatening situations that involve stoppage of breathing. The dangers of prolonged submersion, electrical shock, and carbon monoxide poisoning are of special concern to the boatman.

Weak swimmers and nonswimmers should wear a life-saving device at all times when on or about the water, and precautions should be taken to prevent "man overboard" accidents.

Extreme care must be exercised around boats in handling electrical tools or appliances that are operated by current from shore-based powerlines. Even low voltage systems can produce a fatal shock when directly grounded to the water.

Carbon monoxide poisoning aboard powerboats is most frequently caused by leaky exhaust pipes and fittings that allow engine fumes to escape into cabins or compartments. Cases of monoxide gas poisoning have also occurred in the open cockpits of cabin cruisers and auxiliary sailboats while under power and moving downwind. With boat speed and wind speed approximately the same, exhaust fumes may be drawn up and over the transom and into the aftersection of the boat.

When heaters, other than the electric and catalytic type, are used to warm up enclosed cabin areas, they should be equipped with flues to carry off the smoke and fumes, and the cabin should be kept ventilated at all times in order to replenish the oxygen supply. Charcoal cookers and heaters without flues are especially hazardous in enclosed areas. Since little smoke or flame is noted, the tasteless and odorless but deadly carbon monoxide can quickly change a small, poorly ventilated cabin into a gas chamber.

Victims of accidents or sudden illnesses, such as heart failure, who stop breathing or have difficulty in breathing need immediate help. They may turn blue (or cherry red in the case of gas poisoning) and quickly lose consciousness. Because of its simplicity and effectiveness, the mouth-to-mouth method of resuscitation is recommended for all cases requiring artificial respiration. It can be done immediately after rescue—even in the water if necessary—and does not depend upon special equipment for its application. If the directions given below are carefully followed, the lungs of a nonbreathing victim can be, in most cases, adequately ventilated.

1. Quickly clear the mouth of any foreign matter that might be visible.

2. Tilt the head back so that the chin is pointing upward.

This maneuver should provide for an open airway by moving the tongue away from the back of the throat. (If additional clearance is needed later, it may be necessary to pull or push the jaw upward into a jutting-out position.)

3. Open your mouth wide and place it tightly over the mouth of the victim. Pinch the victim's nostrils shut and blow into his mouth. If the airway is clear, only a moderate resistance to the blowing effort is felt, and the victim's chest will visibly expand.
4. Remove your mouth and allow the air to escape. Repeat the blowing effort.

For an adult, blow vigorously at the rate of about 12 breaths per minute. For a child, take relatively shallow breaths 20 times a minute. On infants, place your mouth over the victim's mouth and nose and give shallow puffs of air about 20 times a minute.

If resistance to the blowing effort is experienced, recheck the head position and hold the jaw forward.

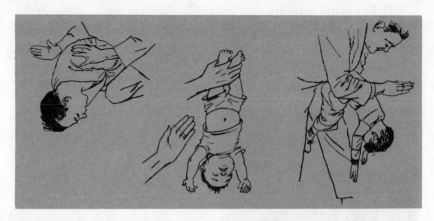

Should the airway remain blocked, quickly turn the victim on his side and administer several sharp blows between the shoulder blades in the hope of dislodging foreign matter. Clear the mouth while the victim is still on his side. Infants and small children should be suspended head downward when an attempt is made to clear the airway.

Keep the victim lying down during and after treatment and avoid chilling or overheating the body. Most successful cases respond in a matter of minutes, but stoppage of breathing caused by electric shock, drugs, and gas poisoning may require ventilation of the lungs for a matter of hours. Medical attention in all instances should be sought as soon as possible.

GLOSSARY OF NAUTICAL TERMS

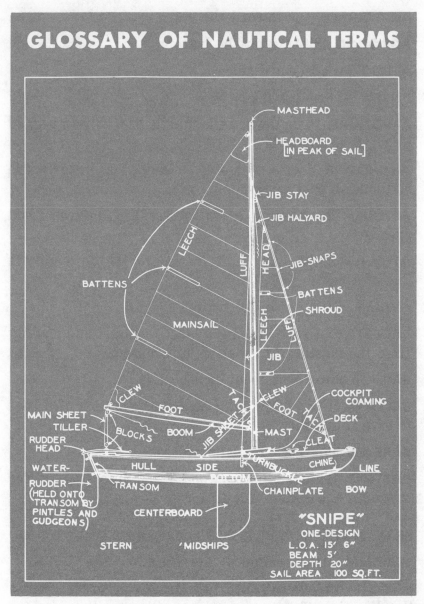

MASTHEAD

HEADBOARD
[IN PEAK OF SAIL]

JIB STAY

JIB HALYARD

JIB-SNAPS

BATTENS

SHROUD

LEECH

LUFF

HEAD

BATTENS

LEECH

LUFF

MAINSAIL

JIB

CLEW

TACK

CLEW

COCKPIT
COAMING

FOOT

FOOT

DECK

MAIN SHEET
TILLER

BLOCKS

BOOM

JIB SHEET

MAST

CLEAT

RUDDER
HEAD

WATER-

HULL

SIDE

TURNBUCKLE

CHINE

LINE

RUDDER
(HELD ONTO
TRANSOM BY
PINTLES AND
GUDGEONS)

TRANSOM

BOTTOM

CHAINPLATE

BOW

CENTERBOARD

STERN

'MIDSHIPS

"SNIPE"
ONE-DESIGN
L.O.A. 15' 6"
BEAM 5'
DEPTH 20"
SAIL AREA 100 SQ.FT.

ABAFT. A relative term used to describe the location of one object in relation to another, in which the object described is farther aft than the other.

ABEAM. The bearing of an object 90 degrees from ahead.

ABOARD. In the boat.

ABOUT. On the other tack.

AFT. At, near, or toward the stern.

AGROUND. Resting on the bottom.

ALEE. To the leeward side.

ALOFT. Above the deck.

AMIDSHIPS. In or toward the middle of a ship in regard to length or breadth.

ANCHOR. A device of metal so shaped as to grip the bottom and hold a vessel.

ASTERN. The bearing of an object 180 degrees from ahead.

ATHWARTSHIPS. At right angles to the fore-and-aft line of a boat.

AWASH. Level with the water.

BACKSTAY. A rope bracing a mast from aft and leading from the masthead to the rail or transom.

BAIL. To throw water out of a boat.

BALLAST. Heavy weights packed in the bottom of a boat to give it stability.

BARE POLES. When no sails are set.

BATTENS. Thin strips of wood fitted into pockets for stiffening the leech of a sail.

BEAM WIND. A wind at right angles to a boat's course.

BEARING. The direction of an object.

BEATING TO WINDWARD. (1) Making progress against the direction of the wind when sailing on the wind or close-hauled. (2) Sailing to windward by zigzag tacks.

BELAY. (1) To make fast to a pin or a cleat. (2) To rescind an order.

BEND. (1) To make fast, e.g., to bend a cable is to make it fast to the anchor. (2) A knot by which a rope is made fast to another.

BIGHT. (1) Any part of a rope except the end; usually refers to a bend in a rope. (2) A cove.

BILGE. The curved part of a boat's hull where the sides and the flat bottom meet.

BITTER-END. The last part of a rope or the last link in an anchor chain.

BLOCK. An apparatus consisting of an outside shell and a sheave through which a rope may be passed.

BOATHOOK. A wooden staff with a metal hook at one end used for fending off or holding on.

BOAT THE OARS. The order to place the oars in the boat.

BOLT-ROPE. The rope around the edge of a sail and to which the sail is sewed.

BOOM. A spar used for extending the foot of a fore-and-aft sail.

BOW. The forward part of a vessel.

BOW PAINTER. The rope secured in the bow of a boat used for securing the boat.

BOWSPRIT. A spar extending forward from the stem and carrying the lead of part of the gear for the head-sails.

BREAST. A mooring or docking line leading at an angle of 90 degrees with the fore-and-aft line of the boat.

BRIDLE. A span of rope with ends secured.

BROACHING TO. To fly into the wind unintentionally; to be thrown broadside on, in surf.

BROAD ON THE BOW. The bearing of an object 45 degrees from ahead.

BROAD ON THE QUARTER. The bearing of an object 135 degrees from ahead.

BUOY. A floating beacon.

CAPSIZE. To overturn.

CAREEN. To list or heel over, usually on a beach.

CARRY AWAY. To break or tear loose.

CAST OFF. To let go.

CATBOAT. A small sailboat with mast stepped well forward and carrying only a mainsail.

CATCH. The point at the beginning of the stroke when the oar takes the water.

CATCH A CRAB. Immersion of the oar during the recovery, thereby causing loss of control of the oar.

CAULK. To fill in the seams with cotton or oakum.

CENTERBOARD. A wooden or metal board carried in a fore-and-aft trunk and capable of being lowered to overcome the leeway of a boat sailing on the wind.

CHAFE. To wear by rubbing.

CHAIN PLATES. Iron or bronze strips bolted to the side of a boat for securing the lower ends of shrouds and stays.

CHOCK. A fitting with jaws that fairlead mooring and anchor lines.

CLAW OFF. Working off a lee shore.

CLEAN. Said of a boat with fine lines.

CLEAT. A fitting of wood or metal with horns, used for securing lines.

CLEW. The after lower corner of a fore-and-aft sail.

CLOSE-HAULED. Sailing close to the wind; same as full-and-by, on the wind, or by the wind.

COAMING. The raised framework about deck openings, and cockpits of open boats.

COCKPIT. The well of a sailing vessel, especially a small boat, for the wheel and the steersman.

COIL. To lay down rope in circular turns.

CORDAGE. A general term for fiber rope of all kinds.

COURSE. The point of the compass toward which the boat is steering.

CRINGLE. A piece of rope spliced into an eye over a thimble in the bolt of a sail.

CRUTCH. The wooden or metal rest for the boom.

DEAD AHEAD. Directly ahead on the extension of the fore-and-aft line of the boat.

DEADRISE. The vertical distance between the keel of a vessel and the turn of the bilge.

DECK BEAM. An athwarthship beam supporting a deck.

DECK HORSE. An athwartship rod for the traveler of a sheet block.

DISMAST. To carry away the mast of a boat.

DISPLACEMENT. The weight of the water displaced by a vessel.

DOUBLE-BANKED. (1) A boat with two men on a thwart. (2) With two men on an oar.

DOWSE. To take in or lower a sail; to put out a light; to cover with water.

DOWNHAUL. (1) A rope led from the head of a headsail and through a block at the foot of the stay for hauling down the sail. (2) Tackle attached to a sliding gooseneck fitting used to adjust the tension along the luff of the sail.

DRAFT. The depth of water to a vessel's keel.

DRIFT. The leeway of a boat or amount of set of a tide or current.

EARING. A short piece of rope secured to a cringle for hauling out the cringle.

EASE OFF. To slack up.

ENSIGN. (1) The national flag. (2) A junior officer in the U.S. Navy.

FAIR-LEADER. An eye to furnish a clear lead.

FAKE DOWN. To coil down a rope so that each fake of rope overlaps the next one underneath, and hence the rope is clear for running.

FALLING OFF. Paying off from the wind.

FATHOM. Six feet.

FEATHER. Turning the blade of an oar horizontally at the finish of a stroke.

FENDER. Canvas, wood, or rope used over the side to protect a boat from chafing.

FEND OFF. To push off when making a landing.

FETCH. To make a windward mark without another tack.

FLARE. The outward and upward curve in the form of a vessel's bow.

FLATTEN IN. To haul in the sheets.

FORE AND AFT. In the direction of the keel.

FOREFOOT. The heel of the stem where it connects to the keel.

FOUL. Jammed, not clear.

FOUND. Equipped.

FRAME. The ribs of a boat strengthening and supporting the shell plating.

FREEBOARD. The distance from the waterline to main deck or gunwale.

FULL-AND-BY. Sailing close-hauled, with all sails full and as close to the wind as possible.

FURL. To gather up and secure a sail or an awning.

GAFF. The spar to which the head of a fore-and-aft sail is secured.

GASKET. A small piece of canvas or line used for furling a sail.

GEAR. The general name for ropes, blocks, and tackles, etc.

GHOSTING. Said of a sailing ship when making very little progress.

GIMBALS. A pair of rings one within the other and with axes at right angles to one another for supporting the compass and maintaining it horizontal.

GROMMET. A ring of rope formed by a single strand laid three times around.

GROUND TACKLE. A term used to cover all of the anchor gear.

GUDGEONS. A support for a rudder consisting of metal braces fastened to the stern post and with eyes to take the pintles of the rudder.

GUNWALE. The upper edge of a boat's side.

GUY. A steadying rope.

GYBE. (Sometimes spelled jibe). When sailing free, to put the helm over so as to bring the boom on the opposite side.

HALLIARDS. Ropes for hoisting gaffs and sails.

HAND TAUT. As tight as can be pulled by hand.

HARD-A-LEE. To put the tiller all the way down.

HEAD-SAILS. Sails forward of the foremast.

HEADSTAY. A forward stay.

HEADWAY. Moving ahead.

HEAVE. To throw.

HEAVE TO. To bring a vessel's head to the wind or sea and hold her there by the use of sails or engines.

HEEL. The lower end; to list over; a vessel turns on her heel when she turns in a short space.

HELM. The tiller.

HOIST. The length of the luff of a fore-and-aft sail.

HOIST AWAY. An order to haul up.

INBOARD. Toward the fore-and-aft center line of the ship.

IN IRONS. To head into the wind and refuse to fall off.

INLAND RULES. The rules of the road enacted by Congress and governing the navigation of inland waters of the United States.

INSHORE. Toward the shore.

IN STAYS. Headed into the wind with all sails shaking.

IRISH PENNANT. An untidy loose end of a rope.

JIB. A headsail set on a stay forward of the foremast.

JIB-HEADED RIG. A rig with all sails triangular.

JURY RIG. A makeshift rig.

KEEL. The timber or bar forming the backbone of the vessel and running from the stem to the sternpost at the bottom of the ship.

KEELSON. The timber bolted on top of the keel and utilized for strengthening the ship's structure.

KETCH. A sailing vessel rigged like a yawl but with the jiggermast forward of the rudder.

KNOCKABOUT. A sloop with jib setting from the stem.

KNOCKED DOWN. The situation of a vessel when listed over by the wind to such an extent that she does not recover.

KNOT. One nautical mile per hour.

LANYARD. A rope made fast to an article for securing it.

LEECH. The after end of a fore-and-aft sail.

LEEBOARD. A board used as a centerboard but secured over the side of a flat-bottomed boat.

LEE HELM. The tiller put to leeward. A vessel carries a lee helm when it is necessary to put the tiller to leeward to hold the course.

LEE SHORE. The land to leeward of the vessel.

LEEWARD. The direction away from the wind.

LEEWAY. The drift of a vessel to leeward caused by the wind or the tide.

LIMBER HOLE. A hole cut in the framing near the keelson to allow water to flow fore-and-aft.

LIST. The athwartship inclination of a vessel due to an excess of weight on one side.

LOCKER. A storage compartment; a clothes wardrobe.

LOOSE-FOOTED. A sail whose foot is not laced to a boom.

LUFF. The forward edge of a fore-and-aft sail.

LUFF HER. An order to bring the vessel into the wind by putting the helm down.

MAINSAIL. The sail spread by the main boom; the lower course on the mainmast.

MARLINE. Two-stranded, left-handed rope, used for fine seizings and for sennit.

MAST. A vertical spar supporting the booms, gaffs, and sails.

MAST STEP. The frame of the keelson into which the heel of a mast is fitted.

MIZZEN. The third mast from forward of a vessel with more than two masts.

MONKEY FIST. A knot worked into the end of a heaving line.

MOORING BUOY. A buoy fitted with a ring and used for mooring a boat.

NUN BUOY. A buoy with a conical top found on the starboard hand on entering a channel and painted red.

OUTBOARD. Toward the sides of the vessel.

OUTHAUL. A rope used for hauling out.

OVERHANG. The projection of the stern beyond the sternpost and of the bow beyond the stem.

PAINTER. A short piece of rope secured in the bow of a small boat, used for making her fast.

PEAK. The upper after corner of a gaff sail.

PEAK HALLIARDS. The lines hoisting the peak of a quadrilateral sail.

PENDANT. A length of rope with a block or a thimble at the end.

PENNANT. A three-sided flag.

PINCH HER. To sail so close to the wind as to allow the sails to shiver.

PINTLE. A bolt of metal secured to the rudder and fitting into the gudgeon, for a swinging support for the rudder.

PITCH POLE. Turned end-over-end in the surf.

POINT. To taper the end of the rope. One of the 32 divisions of the compass card. To head close to the wind.

PORT SIDE. The left side of a vessel looking forward.

PRIVILEGED VESSEL. One which has the right of way.

QUARTER. That portion of a vessel's sides near the stern.

RAKE. The angle of a vessel's masts from the vertical.

REACH. Sailing with a beam wind.

READY ABOUT. An order to prepare for coming about.

REEF. To reduce the area of a sail by making fast reef points and earings.

REEF CRINGLE. A thimble or iron ring spliced in the boltrope on the leech and the luff of fore-and-aft sails in line with the reef points.

RIB. An athwartship frame of a vessel.

RIG. A general description of a vessel's upper works. To set up spars and standing and running rigging of a sailing ship.

RIGGING. Ropes securing masts and sails.

ROACH. The curve of the edge of a sail.

RODE. The anchor line of a small boat.

RUDDER. A flat wooden shape fitted on the stern post by pintles and gudgeons.

RUDDER HEAD. The top of the rudder post.

RUDDER POST. The vertical post upon which the rudder is supported.

RULES OF THE ROAD. Regulations enacted to prevent collisions between ships.

RUNNING BACKSTAYS. Used in a yacht to stay the mast, the weather one being set up and the lee one loosed.

RUNNING RIGGING. That part of a ship's rigging that is movable and rove through blocks, such as halyards and sheets.

SCULL. To propel a boat by working an oar from side to side over the stern.

SEA ANCHOR. A drag (drogue) thrown over the bow to keep a boat to the wind and sea.

SECURE. To make safe.

SEIZE. To bind with small rope.

SET. The direction of the leeway of a vessel or of a tide or current.

SHACKLE. A U-shaped piece of iron or steel with eyes in the ends, closed by a shackle pin.

SHAKE OUT. To let out a reef and hoist the sail.

SHEAVE. The wheel of a block over which the fall of the block reeves.

SHEER. The longitudinal upward curve of a deck. A sudden change of course.

SHEET. The rope used to spread the clew of head-sails and to control the boom of boom sails.

SHIPSHAPE. Neat, seamanlike.

SHORTEN SAIL. To take in or reef some of the sails.

SHROUDS. Side stays of hemp or wire from the masthead to the rail and set up by dead-eyes.

SKEG. The continuation of the keel aft, protecting the propeller and sometimes taking the heel of the rudder.

SLACK. The part of a rope hanging loose. To ease off. The state of the tide when there is no horizontal motion.

SPINNAKER. A light racing triangular sail set on a spinnaker boom on the opposite side of the main boom when sailing free.

SPLICE. To join two ropes together by tucking ends.

SPREADER. A horizontal iron or wooden spar fitted to a mast and used to spread the shrouds and stays.

SQUALL. (1) A brief storm that arrives suddenly. (2) A prolonged gust of wind.

STANDING LUG. A small boat sailing rig in which the sail is set on a yard and the tack is made fast to the mast.

STANDING PART. That part of a line or fall that is secured.

STANDING RIGGING. That part of a ship's rigging that is permanently secured and not movable, e.g., stays, shrouds.

STARBOARD TACK. The tack on which the wind comes over a vessel's starboard side.

STAY. A rope of hemp, wire, or iron used for supporting a mast in a fore-and-aft direction.

STAYSAIL. A sail set upon a stay.

STEM. The timber at the extreme forward part of a boat secured to the forward end of the keel and supporting the bow planks.

STEP. The frame on the keelson into which the heel of a mast fits or stops.

STERN. The after part of the vessel.

STERN FAST, STERN LINE. A rope led over the stern of a vessel and used in securing her by the stern.

STIFF. Said of a vessel when she stands up well without heeling under her sails.

STOVE. Broken in.

STOW. To put in place.

STRAKE. A continuous planking or plating fitted end to end from stem to stern of a boat.

STRETCHERS. Foot braces for oarsmen, consisting of pieces of wood placed athwartships in the bottom of a pulling boat.

STROKE. The sweep of an oar; an order given at the catch of a stroke.

SURGE. To slack suddenly. The heave of the sea.

SWAMP. To sink by filling with water.

SWIVEL. A metal link with an eye at one end fitted so as to swivel and thereby keep turns out of the chain.

TABLING. A broad hem around the edges of a sail.

TACK. The lower forward corner of a fore-and-aft sail. Close-hauled on the wind. To change from one tack to another by putting the helm down.

TACKLE. An arrangement of ropes and blocks to give a mechanical advantage; a purchase.

THIMBLE. An iron ring grooved on the outside for a rope grommet.

THWART. The athwartships seats in a boat.

THWARTSHIPS. At right angles to the fore-and-aft line.

TILLER. A short piece of iron or wood fitting into the rudder head and by which the rudder is turned.

TOPPING LIFT. A rope used for topping up a boom and taking its weight.

121

TOW. To pull through the water. Vessels towed.

TROUGH. The hollow between two waves.

TUMBLE HOME. The amount the sides of a vessel come in from the perpendicular.

TURK'S HEAD. An ornamental knot.

TURNBUCKLE. A metal appliance consisting of a thread and screw capable of being set up or slacked back and used for setting up standing rigging or check stoppers.

TURN OF THE BILGE. The point where the frames of a vessel turn from the vertical to the rounding of the bilge.

TWO BLOCK. When the two blocks of a tackle have been drawn as close together as possible.

UNBEND. To cast adrift or untie.

UNFURL. To cast loose a sail by throwing off the gaskets.

WAKE. A boat's track; behind.

WATERLINE. The line painted on the side of a boat at the water's edge to indicate the proper trim.

WEAR. To change from one tack to another by putting up the helm.

WEATHER. To windward. The state of the atmosphere at a certain time and place.

WEATHER HELM. The tiller put over to windward. A vessel carries a weather helm when it is necessary to put the tiller to windward to hold the course.

WEIGH. To lift the anchor off the bottom.

WHIPPING. A method of preventing the ends of a rope from unlaying or fraying by turns of stout twine with the ends tucked.

WINDWARD. Toward the wind.

WING AND WING. Sailing with booms on opposite sides.

YAW. To steer wildly or out of the line of the course, as when running with a heavy quartering sea.